S0-ANP-384

MUSLIMS AND CHRISTIANS, MUSLIMS AND JEWS

A COMMON PAST, A HOPEFUL FUTURE

Marilyn Robinson Waldman

Editor

Published by

The Islamic Foundation of Central Ohio

in association with

The Catholic Diocese of Columbus
Congregation Tifereth Israel

Columbus, Ohio
1992

Library of Congress Cataloging-in-Publication Data
Muslims and Christians, Muslims and Jews: a common past, a hopeful future / edited by Marilyn Robinson Waldman.
viii & 116 pp. 15.24 x 22.86 cm.
Includes bibliographical references.
ISBN 0-9632668-0-2: $3.00
1. Islam--Relations--Christianity. 2. Christianity--Relations--Islam. 3. Islam--Relations--Judaism. 4. Judaism--Relations--Islam. I. Waldman, Marilyn Robinson. II. Islamic Foundation of Central Ohio. III. Catholic Church. Diocese of Columbus (Ohio). IV. CongregationTifereth Israel (Columbus, Ohio).
BP172.M825 1992 92-20952
297' .1972--dc20 CIP

To all of the children of Abraham

who want to live as friends and neighbors.

**MUSLIMS AND CHRISTIANS, MUSLIMS AND JEWS
A COMMON PAST, A HOPEFUL FUTURE**

Table of Contents

PART III. SOCIETY: THE RELIGIOUS COMMUNITIES IN AMERICA

PREFACE

Marilyn Robinson Waldman

The essays in this volume are revised versions of presentations made at two very successful town-gown conferences in Columbus, Ohio, March 19, 1989, and March 25, 1990. The conferences were entitled "Muslims and Jews: A Common Past, A Hopeful Future," and "Muslims and Christians: Common Themes, Distinctive Identities." Like this volume, each of the conferences was made possible in part by a grant from the Ohio Humanities Council and the National Endowment for the Humanities.

The first conference was co-sponsored by Congregation Tifereth Israel and the Islamic Foundation of Central Ohio. Additional sponsors included three units at The Ohio State University--the Melton Center for Jewish Studies, the Middle East Studies Center, and the Center for Comparative Studies in the Humanities. The second conference was co-sponsored by the Islamic Foundation of Central Ohio and the Catholic Diocese of Columbus, in cooperation with the Metropolitan Area Church Board, and with the help of a grant from the Columbus Foundation.

This volume is, then, the result of exemplary cooperation and collaboration among a variety of groups and individuals. Special thanks go to Dr. Mazhar Jalil, for his wise advice and his tireless efforts on behalf of human understanding; to Toni Mortimer and Amy Waldman, for their editorial assistance; to Artemis S. Leontis for her cover design; and to the Coalition for the Advancement of Jewish Education, which printed similar versions of the "Jews and Muslims" essays in the Winter 1992 issue of *Jewish Education News*. The special focus of that issue was "Judaism and Islam: Fostering Understanding," and it was co-edited by Helena Schlam and Marilyn Robinson Waldman.

According to the planners of the conferences that led to this publication, the purpose of their project was to inform the general community about the historical, religious, ethical, and social commonalities of American Christians, Jews, and Muslims; to lessen the ignorance that leads to intolerance, fear, and strife; and to inform the media in a way that would contribute to reasonable and balanced reporting and editorializing. We offer this volume in the same spirit, and are proud to be able to share the results of the project with a wider audience.

GREETINGS FROM THE SPONSORS

Sohail Khan
President, The Islamic Foundation of Central Ohio

The events that have led to this volume constitute a giant step in creating understanding and respect among the people of these three great religions. In reality, our self-interests do not have to be mutually exclusive. We are all creatures of our Creator, be it God or Allah; we are all descendants of Abraham; we all wish to live in peace, prosperity, happiness, and security. It is not necessary to acquire these conditions at the expense of others. That is, we do not have to deny peace, prosperity, happiness, and security to others in order to have them for ourselves.

As Americans partaking of the fruits of our country, we have the opportunity to help others. It must start here with us. As human beings we have a responsibility and an obligation to help all other human beings, whether in South America, the Middle East, or Africa, achieving better and more humane living conditions. We must realize the human race is all one family and we are all on the same side.

We live in an affluent society. Our energies do not need to be directed toward our survival. There is no threat to our security. We have food, we have prosperity, we have resources. What we lack is the right attitude and trust. Since ignorance breeds fear, foreign cultures, that is, those cultures we know little about, are frequently suspect.

This volume, and the years of cooperation that have made it possible, should be the springboard toward achieving greater understanding, tolerance, and acceptance of other religions, cultures, and traditions. I hope that we do not stop here.

James A. Griffin
Bishop of Columbus

I am happy to greet those who will read this volume, and to offer my own words of introduction.

When Pope John Paul II visited Morocco in 1985, he said, "Generally, Christians and Muslims have understood each other badly." He went on to say, "God is calling us today to change our old habits. We have to respect each other and stimulate each other in good works upon the path of God."

It is my sincere hope that this collection of essays will help foster that understanding and respect, and will help Christians and Muslims to know each other as fellow-travelers on the path of God.

Harold J. Berman
Rabbi, Congregation Tifereth Israel

It was a long time ago that I first became involved in the projects that have led to this volume. Through this experience I have made some good friends and have learned a great deal, not only about Islam, but also about Judaism and the life of the Jewish community.

In the pages that follow, many things are said about Abraham and Isaac and Ishmael, but one story is particularly meaningful to me. It is a story about the end of Abraham's life, the last story. Abraham died and Isaac and Ishmael, who had moved in very different directions and traveled in very different circles, according to the story in the Torah, came together and buried their father. A similar story is also told about Esau and Jacob, who had also moved in different directions and came together to bury their father.

The story has always inspired me because we can see the touching scene, that people who have taken on different definitions of themselves can still come together in times of crisis when comfort is needed to stand together and face both the past and the future. For that reason, the story inspires me, but in the same way it also troubles me. Far too often people do come together when there is a crisis, a particular need, but fail to come together when they could be building a better future.

Today we feel a need for a measure of comfort and sharing in a very troubled world. At the same time we hope that we can learn from the story, that it should not be only crisis and need that bring us together. God willing we will be brought together to learn from each other, to become better friends with each other, and to contribute to building a better future for us all. May God bless us as we try to learn from our traditions and try to learn from each other, and may God grant us that great distinction in the world that we may be makers of peace for our own peoples and for all people.

PART I

RELIGION:
COMMON THEMES IN
BIBLE AND QUR'AN

ON SCRIPTURE AND ITS EXEGESIS: THE ABRAHAM-ISHMAEL STORIES IN THE TORAH AND THE QUR'AN

Reuven Firestone

As both a university professor and a congregational rabbi, I find that I wear two different hats when approaching religious literature. At the university, I attempt to read religious texts from the standpoint of the objective scholar. I look at the Bible, for example, from a number of different angles, but I am always wary of reading it through the particularist lens of a religious tradition. My reference to the "particularist lens of a religious tradition" applies to the phenomenon in which religious dogma determines the manner in which sacred Scripture is read and interpreted.

A classic example of this phenomenon is the variance in Jewish and Christian readings of Isaiah 7:14: ASSUREDLY, MY LORD WILL GIVE YOU A SIGN OF HIS OWN ACCORD! LOOK, THE YOUNG WOMAN IS WITH CHILD AND ABOUT TO GIVE BIRTH TO A SON. LET HER NAME HIM IMMANUEL. BY THE TIME HE LEARNS TO REJECT THE BAD AND CHOOSE THE GOOD, PEOPLE WILL BE FEEDING ON CURDS AND HONEY.[1] Jewish tradition understands the text as a sign of God's unhappiness regarding a decision of the rulers of Israel, while Christian tradition reads it as God's sign of the future virgin birth of Jesus (see Matthew 1:23).

One common practice found in religious exegesis, or interpretation, is that of assigning a new meaning to an old text. New interpretive meanings often become necessary as the ideas of the religion evolve and change. Sometimes, a new interpretive meaning may even be inserted awkwardly into a text which would not appear to provide that meaning. According to the standards of academic scholarship, which seeks to uncover what is assumed to have been the original intent of the text examined, religions tend to read their sacred texts subjectively, that is, through the shaping lens of religious dogma.

In contrast to my activities as an academic, however, I find that as a rabbi to my congregation, I read and interpret religious texts largely through the eyes and lenses of Jewish tradition. As a member of the Jewish clergy, I am an active participant in a long tradition of subjective religious interpretation. I delve deeply into the particularist Jewish styles of textual interpretation in order to derive moral or spiritual lessons, and I may even insert meaning into Scripture homiletically in order to derive a new lesson.

In an ecumenical and educational religious forum such as this collection of essays, neither the dry academic approach nor the subjective approach of any single religious tradition is satisfactory. To read a text only in one traditional religious mode--that is, for example, only through the lenses of Jewish tradition, is to withhold the respect due to other religious traditions such as Islam or Christianity. But to read a religious text only as an "objective" academic exercise also misses the point. That is, to reduce religion to nothing more than an instinctual universal human response to the unknown denies the unique spiritual reality of each and every individual tradition. A third approach must be considered which affirms the particularism of religious exegesis while at the same time transcends its tendency toward insularity or xenophobia. What follows represents an experiment in this enterprise, based on the divergent Jewish and Islamic readings of the story of Abraham and Ishmael.

Before beginning our examination of the topic at hand, however, I wish to stress an observation about monotheism. The "theism" of monotheism tends to be treated in great detail by all monotheistic religions, but the "mono," meaning "one," tends to have been taken for granted since the elimination of polytheism in the Middle East and in the West. That is to say, all expressions of monotheism agree in the existence of only one deity, however that deity may be understood and defined among the great variety of monotheistic theologies. The "mono" of monotheism, however, is invariably applied by each religious tradition as firmly to *itself* as it is to God. It is expressed by all monotheistic religions in the following way: "There is only one God, and God has affirmed for us that there is only one true religion--our religion."

Monotheism is, by definition, exclusivist. God is the exclusive object of worship. But the religious institutions professing monotheism are also exclusivist. Each claims that, just as there is only one God, God has chosen it to bring God's message to all humankind. In common speech, the message is that there is only one "true religion," and that is . . . "our religion." It should be noted that this sense of absolutism in self-definition is expressed within as well as among the three great monotheistic traditions. Each has its own internal bickering as to which expression of Judaism or Christianity or Islam, is the "true" religion.

With this attribute of monotheistic exclusivism in mind, we realize that though there are many holy books in this world, monotheism demands that there be only one true Scripture. The logic of monotheism insists that one God could not have given three or more different and sometimes even contradictory scriptures. Only one scripture can be true Scripture. For Jews, it is the *Tanakh*, or Hebrew Bible, and most specifically that divinely revealed section known as the Torah, revealed to the people of God's covenant: the Jews. For Christians, it is the New Testament, the proof of the New Covenant obtaining between God and Christians: those who witness the reality of Jesus as the Messiah and the Salvation of humankind. For Muslims, it is the holy Qur'an, the final and perfect revelation given through the last and final prophet Muhammad, to the early Arab Muslims, and taught to the "true believers": the *umma*, or community of Islam.

All monotheistic religions approach other religions' holy books through lenses formed by their own Scripture and tradition. Two important considerations apply here. The first is that older scripture is interpreted through the lenses of newer scripture. Christians, for example, read the "Old Testament" through the hermeneutic of the New Testament. To use my now familiar metaphor, they read and interpret it through the particularist lenses of their own religious tradition. Similarly, Muslims see the *Tawrat* (Torah) and the *Injiil* ("Evangelikon" or New Testament) through the lenses of religious tradition established by the Qur'an. No religion reads any scripture "objectively," without being profoundly influenced by the claims of its own religious tradition.

The second rule is that newer claims for sacred scripture can never be acceptable to older traditions if the new claims were made after the canonization of the earlier scripture. Once the boundaries are established, they cannot be broken. Christians, therefore, cannot accept the Qur'an as revelation. And Jews can accept neither the New Testament nor the Qur'an. Each of the monotheistic traditions agrees that there can be no God but God, but each also insists that there can be no true or accurate revelation but the "real," that is . . . "our" revelation.

With all this in mind, we can begin to understand the natural difficulty that adherents of Western monotheistic religions have in truly respecting the sacred scripture of other religions. It is difficult for even the most open-minded to escape the feeling that s/he is observing in another Scripture a mistaken presumption, a misinterpretation of God's true design. It is, for this very reason, necessary to try as best we can to remove our particularist lenses if we wish to engage in a truly open and fruitful discussion across the exegetical boundaries of religious traditions. We shall try to do just that as we examine two recognizably similar but quite different tellings of the story of Abraham and Ishmael.

Many of us are familiar with the journeys and activities of Abraham found in the Hebrew Bible. He left Ur of the Chaldees with his father, and journeyed to Haran (in today's southern Turkey), where his father died. From Haran, he journeyed along with his wife Sarah and nephew Lot to a land known as *eretz kana'an*, the Land of the Canaanites, in response to God's command. Aside from a brief sojourn in Egypt, the Bible depicts Abraham thereafter living a nomadic life within the area known later in the Bible as *eretz yisra'el*, the Land of the Israelites. He never again leaves his new land, the land promised by God to him and his offspring. While in Egypt, however, according to Jewish tradition but not explicity mentioned in the Bible, Hagar was given as a handmaid to Abraham's wife Sarah.

Abraham proceeds to have a number of adventures until we arrive at Chapter 16 of Genesis. Now we must realize that any retelling of a story, whether translation or paraphrase, is an interpretation of that story. By our choice of words or even inflection, we emphasize or deemphasize various aspects, unconsciously as well as knowingly, whenever we re-tell a story. With that caveat in mind, we shall continue the narrative.

Sarah cannot become pregnant, so she gives her Egyptian handmaid, Hagar, to Abraham so that he will attain progeny through her. After Hagar becomes pregnant, a serious family conflict develops between the two women. Sarah, the woman with higher social status, treats Hagar so harshly that she flees into the desert, where she meets an angel of God. The angel commands Hagar to return to Sarah, and gives Hagar a somewhat enigmatic prophecy regarding her future son, Ishmael, whose offspring will be innumerable. Hagar returns and Ishmael is born.

In Chapter 17, the covenant between Abraham and God is reaffirmed through the act of circumcision. Ishmael is circumcised along with Abraham's entire male household. God also promises Abraham a son through Sarah, and informs him that the covenant will be attained only through Isaac--not through Ishmael. But God also assures Abraham that Ishmael will father a great nation, begetting twelve princes.

Chapter 18 is the story of the three visitors to Abraham, who tell him in Sarah's presence of their future son who will be born the following year. The visitors then set out to destroy the cities of Sodom and Gemorah.

When the story returns to the occasion of Isaac's birth in Chapter 21, we learn that Isaac is born and circumcised. At Isaac's weaning celebration a year or so later, however, the smoldering conflict between Sarah and Hagar bursts forth into a full-scale fight. Abraham is deeply saddened by this, but God instructs him to follow Sarah's wishes. Sarah thereupon decides to banish Hagar and Ishmael, so Abraham rises early and sends them off with provisions which are soon spent in the desert.

Hagar sets Ishmael down under a bush and walks far enough away so that she will not hear the cries of her son dying of thirst, for she cannot bear the pain. She sits down and cries. But God hears the voice of Ishmael and sends an angel who confirms God's promise that Ishmael will become a great nation. God provides a well for them and also continues to provide for the boy as he grows up in the desert of Paran.

This is essentially the end of Ishmael's story in the Bible. A brief comment can be found in Genesis 25:9, where Ishmael joins with Isaac in burying their father Abraham. The names of Ishmael's twelve sons are also listed there, along with the statement that Ishmael lived to the age of 137.

Nothing more can be found of Ishmael in the Hebrew Bible. A few references to him can be found in the New Testament, with one striking allegory found in Galatians 4:21-31. The New Testament references, however, provide no additional insight into Ishmael's life.

The Qur'an, however, provides important additional information about Abraham and Ishmael. Because the Qur'an is not organized by chronology as is most of the Hebrew Bible, no single section will provide a full accounting of their story. References to Abraham and Ishmael must therefore be collected from a variety of chapters and contexts.

Qur'an 14:37 mentions that Abraham caused some of his offspring to live in a desolate valley next to God's sacred House in order to establish regular prayer. While the location of that sacred place is not given here, Qur'an 3:96 teaches that the first house of worship provided for humankind was at the blessed Bakka, a synonym say the Muslim commentators, for the sacred city of Mecca (pronounced "Makka" in Arabic). The Qur'an continues in the following verse to tell us that the famous *maqam ibrahim*--the station of Abraham--is located in that place. In Mecca today can be found a Station of Abraham within the Sacred Compound, in which lies the Ka'ba, the sacred ritual center of Islam. The Qur'an explains further that this is the place to which the Pilgrimage, the Hajj, is a religious obligation. In fact, Qur'an 2:124-29 depicts Abraham and Ishmael raising up the foundations of the Ka'ba and purifying it for the Pilgrimage and for prayer.

How did Abraham get to Mecca? The Qur'an does not tell us. It rather assumes that those hearing or reading the Qur'an already know the answer. And indeed, traditional Islamic exegesis recalls ancient legends explaining how Abraham came to Mecca. The following legend can be found in most of the authoritative Qur'an commentaries and is told on the authority of one of the most respected early Qur'an commentators, 'Abdallah ibn 'Abbas, known as the father of qur'anic exegesis.

Although no biblical verses are quoted, nor is the Bible ever referred to, the legend is immediately recognizable to those familiar with the biblical story of the tragic conflict between Sarah and Hagar. As in Genesis 21:14,

Abraham gives Hagar provisions for her journey; but in the Islamic legend, Abraham leaves Sarah and the land of the Canaanites and personally brings Hagar and Ishmael to the desert location of the future holy city of Mecca. Abraham deposits them under a thorned tree next to the location of the future Ka'ba, reminiscent of Hagar's leaving Ishmael under the bush in Genesis 21:15. Abraham then begins his long journey home, but Hagar follows and asks to whom Abraham is entrusting them in such a desolate place. After a long silence, he answers, "to God." Abraham then recites this prayer found in Qur'an 14:37: O LORD! I HAVE MADE SOME OF MY OFFSPRING LIVE IN AN UNCULTIVATED VALLEY BY YOUR SACRED HOUSE, IN ORDER, O LORD, THAT THEY ESTABLISH REGULAR PRAYER.

Ishmael is only an infant at the time, and when the water in Hagar's waterskin is depleted, she becomes dehydrated and her milk stops flowing for her son. As Ishmael's thirst becomes unbearable, he begins writhing or having a seizure. Hagar cannot bear to see him die, so she leaves him under the bush and climbs a nearby hill looking for help. When none is to be found, she runs across to the opposite hill and looks from there, but sees nothing. She runs between the two hills seven times. Desperate, she finally hears a voice and runs back to her son, whom she sees is accompanied by an angel, often named in the text as Gabriel. He brings forth water from the ground for them and Hagar dams up the flow and scoops it into her waterskin, thus saving the life of her son. The angel then tells Hagar that the boy and his father will one day build the House of God at that very spot.

According to Muslims, the well that the angel brought forth is called Zamzam, and is the very well within today's Sacred Precinct at Mecca, the well from which today's pilgrims drink when they make the Hajj to Mecca and its environs. The hills between which Hagar ran searching for help, are the famous hills of Safa and Marwa in Mecca, and every Muslim pilgrim ritually re-enacts Hagar's running between them seven times even today when participating in the Hajj.

The story is not over, however, for after Hagar and Ishmael are established in Mecca, a group from the Arab tribe of Jurhum happens by and notices signs of life in what was thought to be a desolate and dry valley. They send a scout, who finds Hagar and Ishmael near the sacred well. The tribal leaders ask permission of Hagar to settle with them there, which is granted, and they then bring their families to Mecca. As Ishmael grows up, he learns the Arabic language and culture from the Jurhum tribe, and eventually marries one of the Jurhumite women.

This might be an appropriate ending to the legend as well, but in fact it continues, for Abraham is not satisfied that he left his oldest son alone with Hagar in the desert, despite the fact that he knows God will be with the boy (as in Genesis 21:20). As a loving and responsible father who has not rejected his eldest son, he feels the need to check up on him, so he journeys to Mecca. Ishmael is away from home at the time, but Abraham meets Ishmael's wife. She is inhospitable, rude, and downright mean to Abraham (who represents the very epitome of hospitality in both Jewish and Islamic tradition). Abraham gives her a message for Ishmael: "divorce your wife," in a code she cannot understand. He then proceeds on his return journey homeward. Upon Ishmael's return, he immediately senses that his father was there, and asks his wife what has happened. She innocently tells him about a strange and ugly old man who came by, and Ishmael knows from the coded message that he must divorce her. He then marries another woman from the Jurhum tribe.

A while later, Abraham once again feels the need to check up on his son. Ishmael is again away when he arrives, but this time Abraham is received with wonderful hospitality and respect by Ishmael's new wife. Abraham then asks her to give Ishmael the coded message that his wife is the proper choice. They have children, and through a long genealogy not provided in this legend but connected to the legend by other Islamic sources, we come to realize that the ultimate result of this divinely sanctioned match (through the prophet Abraham) is the birth of Muhammad, the last and greatest of all prophets.

Abraham visits Mecca a third time. This time he finds Ishmael at home, trimming arrows in the shade of the same tree under which Abraham left him and his mother so many years before. Abraham informs Ishmael that God has given him a command. Ishmael replies that if God has commanded anything to Abraham, he is obligated to carry it out. Abraham then informs Ishmael of God's command to them both to build God's house, the sacred Ka'ba, as in Qur'an 2:127. They both follow the divine commandment, and Ishmael hands his father the stones as Abraham sets them in place on God's House. As they build, they pray the verse found in Qur'an 2:127: OUR LORD, ACCEPT [THIS] FROM US, FOR YOU ARE THE ALL-HEARING, THE ALL-KNOWING.

We have in the Jewish and the Islamic tellings of the Abraham-Ishmael story two different, and in many respects contradictory versions, each based upon a different sacred scripture. According to the biblical view, God's covenant with Abraham is established with Isaac, not the rejected Ishmael. Isaac has a son named Jacob, who is subsequently renamed Israel by God's angel, and he fathers the twelve tribes who will make up the Israelite people. The covenant is established with Isaac--not Ishmael. Isaac is a willing Sacrifice to God on Mt. Moriah, the very location of the future Temple in Jerusalem--God's House. Abraham's progeny will include David, the greatest king of Israel, and the symbol for unity and salvation of the Jewish people.

But according to the qur'anic view, Abraham personally brings his oldest son Ishmael, never rejected, to the sacred site of Mecca. It is in Mecca that they will build the House of God. And Abraham is careful to see to it that Ishmael marries a proper woman who will be worthy of the status of matriarch, mothering the genealogical line that will result in Muhammad, the greatest prophet and the vehicle for God's greatest gift, the Qur'an.

According to Jewish tradition, Ishmael's history became irrelevant to the sacred history of God's people. God's sacred design in history rests in the line of Isaac. But according to Islamic tradition, Ishmael is the progenitor of God's greatest prophet who would one day lead his people to establish God's rule on earth. Sacred history rests in the line of Ishmael.

Now here is a classic case of two religious traditions telling different and even competing stories about the same paradigmatic characters. This observation is not new. Ever since ancient times, adherents of various religions knew that other religions perceived history and the path to salvation differently, and they often discussed, argued, disputed, and even committed violence over their disagreements.

Every monotheistic religious tradition has evolved its own exclusivist defense against the claims of others. Jewish tradition has tended to consider the Islamic claims to be mistakes or attempts to distort religious truth in the name of temporal power. Islamic tradition has tended to consider Jewish claims to be the result of tampering with the text of the Torah, which originally contained a clear prophecy telling of the coming of Muhammad and the rise of Islam. Both have considered their scripture coeval with Creation. Contradictory claims cannot be tolerated. There can only be one TRUTH. Somebody has got it right, and the others have got it wrong. And one knows who's who.

The classic academic approach would be to analyse the text of both traditions and try to determine if one tradition may have "borrowed" from the other, or to try to determine if they both may have evolved out of a common tradition. It would break down and analyse each unit of each rendition of the legend to try to extract its secrets. This tendency toward reductivism among academic approaches has the effect of reducing the power of the legends to merely the sum of simple, even mediocre parts. It tends to ignore the unique literary qualities of the different versions and the truths that legends such as these provide.

A different approach to competing religious claims such as these is needed, but not one based on theological doctrine. I have heard religious thinkers, for example, devise intricate theological devices to solve mutually-exclusive doctrinal problems such as the example discussed here. But these attempts tend to remain unsatisfactory to at least one, and often both parties to the conflict. I have also heard the common defeatist, atheistic view that the contradictory claims do nothing more than demonstrate the arbitrariness of religion, showing that religion can only grasp at straws to explain human and natural phenomena.

An alternative approach to competing, even contradictory religious beliefs such as the example given here with Abraham, Isaac, and Ishmael, might serve to stimulate some discussion about the process of interreligious dialogue. This approach would require, first of all, that we be willing to acknowledge that we will never determine the "original" text. Jews claim that the Torah is chronologically older than the Qur'an. The qur'anic stories of biblical characters therefore, must be variants (i.e., mistaken versions or distortions) of biblical stories. According to this view, the Islamic telling of the Abraham story is a conscious distortion of the Bible in order to justify the later claim that Islam is God's favored religion.

Muslims, however, claim that the Qur'an was never created, but actually preceded Creation. It existed before the giving of the Torah on Mt. Sinai. And since the "true" story once existed also in biblical revelation, Jewish religious leaders once knew of Ishmael's chosen status, but consciously distorted their scripture in order to justify the claim that Judaism is God's favored religion. Both claim the "original" and therefore "correct" story.

But modern studies in literary theory challenge both views. It has become evident that early stories on biblical themes have been found in a number of ancient civilizations, from Mesopotamia to Egypt, which pre-date the biblical tellings. It appears, in fact, that there never was an "original" telling of the Abraham story in the literary sense. The legends have existed in various forms since time immemorial. No religion can claim exclusive ownership or the right to an exclusive "truth" in this regard.

The answer to the question of which is the "original" text is simple: it is the wrong question. Arguments over "which came first" can never be resolved. They are counterproductive. They do not promote dialogue and understanding--only polemics and dispute. We must overcome the need to figure out "who was right," and move on to more important issues.

Second, we must be willing to respect the religious drives of those coming out of different paths to God. We all need the personal and religious confidence to stake our efforts on the assumption that something cherished by intelligent and sensitive people over many generations is at least unlikely to be trivial. More likely, it contains great truths from which we may also learn.

For me as a religious Jew having grown up believing in the reality of God's covenant with the Jewish people, the Islamic telling of the Abraham-Ishmael story presents a challenge--not to my beliefs, but to my smugness, to my general attitude toward other religions. Studying the Islamic approach does not cause me to abandon my beliefs. On the contrary, it opens my eyes to understand that Muslims, like Jews, see themselves in a special relationship with God in their acting-out of God's commandments. As I come to understand the depth of this relationship, I come to respect and value the spirituality and religious imperative of my Muslim colleagues, even though I am coming from a different place.

This is not to say that religious truth is only relative. God does not change. God is one and is eternal. But human perceptions and understandings of God differ, and our perceptions are affected by many things, including language, culture, technology, and history. Jews and Muslims act on what is believed to be God's demands upon them. As we learn to respect the religiosity and spirituality of each other's traditions at the same time that we affirm the depth and meaning of our own, we need no longer suffer the affront nor the anger when we note the differences between us.

In the case of the Abraham-Isaac-Ishmael story, Jews and Muslims cannot resolve the question of whether God's blessing to Abraham passed to Isaac or Ishmael. But that question is the wrong question. We must ask ourselves, rather, how to accept the fact that we have different, even sometimes contradictory, assumptions, and beliefs, and still work together for mutual benefit.

We need not try to convince each other to agree with each other's religious views. We need not seek converts. And we need not try to create a new hybrid religion of Judaism and Islam. We should rather note these differences at the same time that we affirm our commonalities. When Jews and Muslims work together and learn more about one another, even if for limited periods of time, we promote contact and discussion about interests that we do have in common, and we learn that some of the negative assumptions we have had about each other are not borne out in fact. We learn to eliminate many of the stereotypes and subsequently learn to deal with the important issues in a new and more constructive manner. Each group need only offer the respect that is due to ancient traditions and religious beliefs, and expect the same in return.

In this shrinking world with greater intermingling between religions and cultures, in an age when the term "global village" has become an accurate description of modern life, every group must learn to accept differences at the same time that it believes in its own way. Whether Abraham's blessing passed to Isaac or Ishmael is a question that cannot be reconciled by Jews and Muslims. The question is, can we accept the fact that we have different assumptions and beliefs and still live together? In the world of interreligious dialogue, the term "mutual respect" is the key. Not "right" or "wrong." With this in mind, the children of Ishmael and the children of Isaac, all the children of Abraham, will be able to work together here and abroad in order to build a future beneficial to all.

ENDNOTE

[1]Throughout this volume, direct quotations from scriptures appear in capital letters.

SUGGESTIONS FOR FURTHER READING

Firestone, Reuven. *Journeys in Holy Lands: The Evolution of the Abraham-Ishmael Legends in Islamic Exegesis*. Albany, NY, 1990.

Peters, Francis E. (ed.). *Judaism, Christianity, and Islam: The Classical Texts and Their Interpretation*. Princeton, NJ, 1990.

Waldman, Marilyn Robinson. "New Approaches to 'Biblical' Material in the Qur'an." *The Muslim World* 75 (1985):1-16.

REUVEN FIRESTONE is a Yad HaNadiv research fellow in Jewish and Islamic Studies at the Hebrew University in Jerusalem, Israel. He received his Ph.D. in Near Eastern Languages and Literatures from New York University (1988), and his Rabbinic Ordination from Hebrew Union College (1982).

MUSLIMS, JEWS, AND THE ABRAHAMIC CONNECTION

Jamal A. Badawi

My brethren, cousins, I greet you with the Islamic greeting, "May the peace, blessing, and mercy of Allah Almighty be with you all."

This essay takes an uncommon approach to "the Abrahamic connection" between Muslims and Jews. Many scholars have written about what the Qur'an says about that connection, but the other side has remained largely unexplored, i.e., whether there may be something in the Bible that refers to commonality between Muslims and Jews. That is my theme.

In talking about biblical indications of commonality, I am going to refer to three great prophets: Abraham, Moses, and Isaiah, and to try to see within these three great prophets some aspects of the forthcoming of Prophet Muhammad (Peace be upon him!). Beginning with Prophet Abraham, we are told in Genesis 12:2-3 that God promised to bless all the nations of the earth through the descendants of Abraham. At that time, ironically, Abraham did not have any children.

Then we are told in Genesis 16 that Abraham (since his first wife Sarah was barren) was married to another wife, and that wife was the handmaid of Sarah, Hagar. We are told then that Sarah mistreated Hagar, so Hagar ran away. An angel appeared to her and told her that she was pregnant and that she would give birth to a child, and the name was given by the angel as Isma'il--Ishmael, with the promise that God would multiply him exceedingly. Hagar returned and gave birth to the first son of Abraham, Ishmael.

After the birth of Ishmael, who remained, by the way, the only son of Abraham for nearly fourteen years, and before the birth of Isaac, even in Genesis 17:4, we are told that the promise of God to place Ishmael's nation on earth was reiterated. Subsequently, we are told that the first wife of Abraham, Sarah, gave birth to Isaac, the second son of Abraham. In Genesis 21, we are told how God promised to bless Isaac and made His covenant with him. But in the meantime, in verses 13 and 18, we are told that Ishmael was also promised a blessing and that God would make of him a great nation.

According to the Bible, Abraham took Hagar and Ishmael to live in the wilderness of Paran (Genesis 21:21). Now, when did this happen? Did this take place before the birth of Isaac or afterwards? Was it because of the jealousy of Sarah, or was it part of the divine plan to raise a prophet in this desert land? It is a matter where there could be differences of understanding, but there is one thing that there seems to be a great deal of agreement upon--that Ishmael and Hagar settled in Paran. Paran, according to the thirteenth-century Arab geographers al-Yaqut and al-Baghdadi, in Arabic is actually the Hijaz, more specifically Mecca.

It was the settlement of Hagar and Ishmael in Mecca that heralded the beginning of a new society or community after the well of Zamzam gushed miraculously under the feet of baby Ishmael while he cried for water. Out of the descendants of Ishmael no doubt came Prophet Muhammad (Peace be upon him!). This is something that has already been acknowledged in, for example, *Dictionary of the Bible* (ed. John B. Davis), *International Standard Bible Encyclopedia* (ed. Geoffrey W. Bromiley), and *Smith's Bible Dictionary* (ed. William Smith). There is growing awareness and realization that indeed Prophet Muhammad is among the descendants of Ishmael. These references in Genesis alone suffice to tie together not only Muslims and Jews, but Muslims, Jews, and Christians as well. The Israelite prophets were descended from the second son of Abraham, Isaac; and Prophet Muhammad came from the descendants of the first son.

Several centuries after Abraham there came a great prophet, Moses (Peace be upon him!). Deuteronomy 18:18, before the death of Prophet Moses (Peace be upon him!), echoes the promise made in Genesis--that God would send from among their brethren a prophet like Abraham. He said that God would put His words in the mouth of that prophet so he would not speak on his own; but what he hears, shall he say.

A number of observations might be made about this phraseology. The word "brethren" can be a reference to other Israelites, but it can also be used in the Bible to refer to the closest kin of the Israelites, as in, for example, Genesis 16:12 and 25:18. Furthermore, among the great prophets in history, there are no two prophets who are so much alike in their history and struggle as Moses and Muhammad (Peace be upon them!):

First of all, both of them were prophets who received a comprehensive code of law, unlike, for example, Jesus (Peace be upon him!), who said that he came not to destroy the law of prophets but to fulfill it. Both Moses and Muhammad, in fact, had to counter the tyranny of rulers at the time.

Second, both of them had to flee their homelands in pursuit of a new base for the establishment of their faith and their identity.

Third, both of them had hot encounters with their enemies in some form or other.

Fourth, both emerged victorious, morally and militarily.

Fifth, both of them were prophets and statesmen at the same time.

And sixth, the promise that God would put His words in the prophet's mouth is an accurate description of how revelation came to Prophet Muhammad (Peace be upon him!), because the Qur'an did not come to him by inspiration so that he used his own words; rather it was dictated by Gabriel, the angel of revelation, exactly word for word, which is God's way of putting His words in the prophet's mouth.

The same book, Deuteronomy (33:2), contains a possible reference to three great prophets, the last three major prophets, in succession, Moses, Jesus, Muhammad (Peace be upon them all!): THE LORD CAME FROM SINAI, AND ROSE FROM SEIR UNTO THEM; HE SHINED FORTH FROM MOUNT PARAN. Later on, some translations indicate that HE CAME WITH TEN THOUSAND SAINTS. "THE LORD CAME FROM SINAI" appears to me to be a reference to Moses' receiving the Torah on Mount Sinai. "AND ROSE FROM SEIR UNTO THEM" reminds one of the Palestinian village which is today called Sa'ir in Arabic--Seir. Other authorities, like al-Yaqut in the thirteenth century, and Ibn Taymiyya in the fourteenth century, also indicated that Sa'ir was a village in Palestine. Could that also be a reference to the second great prophet, Jesus (Peace be upon him!)?

What is more interesting in terms of the relationship between Muslims and Jews is the third phrase "AND HE SHINED FORTH FROM MOUNT PARAN." What is Paran? As was mentioned earlier, in Genesis 21:21 Paran is the place where Abraham took Hagar and Ishmael, and Paran can mean the Hijaz, more specifically, Mecca. In fact, according to Muslims, the pre-Islamic monuments of Mecca still exist: the Ka'ba, built by Abraham with the help of Ishmael his son; the well of Zamzam; and the hills of Safa and Marwa, between which Hagar was running in search of water before the well of Zamzam gushed under the feet of Ishmael.

One might also argue that when the Bible says that God came, rose, and shined forth, it is referring to the three basic stages of divine grace and of the revelation given to prophets: a great change coming through the Torah given to Prophet Moses (Peace be upon him!); additional revelation rising through Jesus (Peace be upon him!); and, as Muslims believe, the finality of the revelation, the completeness and combination of all that is good and noble in the teaching of all the prophets shining forth in the fullness of light through the very last and seal of them, Prophet Muhammad (Peace be upon him!). When the sun comes in the middle of the day, and there is no more light expected, that is the fullness of light. When translations go on to say that God came with ten thousand saints, a Muslim is reminded of the number of Muslims who returned to Mecca victoriously in 630 of the Common Era (CE).

The book of Isaiah contains three interesting references that seem to connect the history of Muslims and Jews, or Moses and Muhammad (Peace be upon them both!). Isaiah 11 tells about a great person who is yet to come from the stem of Jesse. That person is described as having wisdom, understanding, the knowledge of God's righteousness, faithfulness, and also strength; he will be a judge and he will rule in justice against the wicked. The utterances of this prophet or the revelations that he will receive will have a great impact upon humanity, as symbolized by the statement that he will smite the earth with the wrath of his tongue or his mouth. No prophet who came after Isaiah combined all of these characteristics except Prophet Muhammad (Peace be upon Him!). In fact, is Jesse really the father of David, or someone else? According to *Encyclopedia Biblica* (eds. T.K. Cheyne and J.S. Black), Jesse is an abbreviation of Ishmael, in Hebrew, Yishmael, Yeshe, Jesse.

Isaiah 21:13-17 begins with the oracles or utterances, the divine utterances concerning Arabia. It then instructs the people of Tema to welcome those refugees who come to them because of persecution and to support them and protect them in any way they can. It then indicates that in a very short period of time, the glory of Kedar shall diminish and the men of the children of Kedar shall be diminished as well. Where is that land of Tema? Who are those children of Kedar? And was that reference or prophecy ever realized in history?

According to Genesis 25:13, two of the children of Ishmael were named Tema and Kedar, so both Tema and Kedar were "Arabs," i.e., descendants of Ishmael. Furthermore, according to *Dictionary of the Bible* (ed. John Mackenzie), Tema is an oasis north of Medina, to which in 622 CE Prophet Muhammad migrated with the Muslims after persecution in Mecca.

When the passage in Isaiah says that the children of Kedar have diminished, Muslims are reminded of the historic battle, the famous battle of Badr, which took place in the second year after Prophet Muhammad's (Peace be upon him!) migration from Mecca to Medina (624 CE). In that battle Muslims were outnumbered more than three to one and much less well equipped with weapons than their adversaries, but the Qur'an testifies that there was divine intervention. In fact, in that battle seventy of the most cruel persecutors of Muslims were killed and seventy were taken prisoners, in spite of the vast strength that they had. Isaiah also speaks about sharing their bread or defending them with their bread, exactly what happened in this migration when the refugees persecuted in Mecca were received with open arms. The Medinese people received them with a great deal of generosity and shared everything with them and undertook to defend them should an attack come.

Finally, Isaiah 42 (especially up to verse 58), speaks of a great personality, somebody who is called the "elect of God," very similar to the title normally given to Prophet Muhammad (Peace be upon Him!)--Mustafa--the elect one, the servant of God. It indicates that he will give a code of law that is to be obeyed by the islands, or coastlands, that is, to be spread wide and reach many different places; that he will be a person who is loving of civilization and knowledge; and that he will save declining civilization--a dimly burning wick in prophecy--rather than destroy it. He will be a light unto all nations, bringing people forth from darkness into light; and according to Isaiah, God says that He will not give His glory to another, i.e., someone to come after "the elect," and that with "the elect's" coming, there will be a new style of praising God--singing a new song unto the Lord. One method of singing glory to God will be by shouting or by praising the Lord with loud voices from the top of the mountains. Isaiah indicates that God will give His "elect" victory over his adversaries, and that with his coming, joy will come to the villages inhabited by Kedar, and also by the inhabitants of Sela.

Is there a connection between this bibical passage and the coming of Prophet Muhammad (Peace be upon Him!)? To begin with, it says that he will receive the law, that the islands shall wait for his laws. Isaiah came after Moses, and nobody came after Moses with a complete, comprehensive code of laws, but one: that was Prophet Muhammad (Peace be upon Him!). As for the islands, the farthest islands, it is interesting to note that Prophet Muhammad's religion is spread so wide in the world that today one out of five human beings is a Muslim. In fact, the largest Muslim country is not Arab; it is Indonesia, the *island* of Indonesia, with about eighty-five percent of its 176,000,000 inhabitants Muslim. So whether the term, the original term, means islands, coastlands, or drylands, all are applicable to Indonesia.

When God says that His "elect" will rule in justice, that means he will be a prophet and a ruler; and nobody came after Moses with this combination of traits except for Prophet Muhammad (Peace be upon him!). The Bible also indicates that the "elect's" mission will be not only to his own people but also to the nations. From some of the early Meccan revelations to Muhammad, there is an indication of the universality of the message given to him, and of his mandate to unite mankind and follow three previous brother prophets, one might say, under that arch and under the final complete revelation.

This passage in Isaiah also speaks about the "elect's" having victory over his adversaries. The Muslims achieved great victories over the two tyrannical superpowers of the times, the Persian and Byzantine empires.

When the Bible speaks about the fact that he will not extinguish civilization, or the light of learning, Muslims are reminded that the coming of Islam preserved the classical heritage of the Greeks, adding creatively to it and providing resources for later European Renaissance.

The Bible speaks about praising God in a new style and says to sing a new song unto the Lord. Could that possibly be a reference to another language, different from the language of Hebrew, in which previous scriptures were revealed? Could that possibly be a reference to the daily chanting of *adhan*, the Islamic call to prayer, from hundreds of thousands of minarets around the world, and also the chanting of the Qur'an? When the Bible speaks about people praising the Lord from the top of the mountains, could that have any connection to the Muslims, standing every year on Mount Arafat, praising God with the very famous chant they have in pilgrimage?

The Bible says that the children of Kedar, or the villages inhabited by Kedar, shall be joyful with his coming. I have already indicated that the Bible tells us that Kedar is actually the name of a son of Ishmael. Not only this--it says that other people will also be happy with his coming, the people of Sela; and according to some ancient Arab geographers, Sela is actually a mountain near Medina.

Perhaps the most significant connection between Jews and Muslims is the Abrahamic connection. Like many scholars I have studied the Qur'an to see what it says about Abraham and Moses and the commonality among the basic threads of their teaching. I think equal attention should be given to the study of the Bible in a new light, which may perhaps lead us to discover more and more threads of that commonality.

SUGGESTIONS FOR FURTHER READING

Badawi, Jamal A. *Bridgebuilding Between Christian and Muslim*. Newberg, OR, 1982.

____. "Muhammad in the Bible." In *Some Aspects of Prophet Muhammad's Life*. Indianapolis, IN, 1983, 35-57.

JAMAL A. BADAWI is a noted Islamic scholar, author, and lecturer. He is Associate Professor of Management at St. Mary's University, and received his Ph.D. in Personnel Management and Labor Economics from Indiana University (1970).

MARY, MOTHER OF JESUS, IN CHRISTIAN AND ISLAMIC TRADITIONS

R. Marston Speight

The figure of Mary, the Mother of Jesus, as depicted in the Qur'an and the Bible, is one of the important meeting places for Muslims and Christians. When we talk about Mary together, at least in Scriptural terms, we have a fairly clear idea of what the other party is saying. Perhaps the reason for this is that in the Qur'an and Bible, Mary is always referring to someone else or to something else.[1] In the Qur'an, for example, even when Mary's mother holds her newborn girl-child before the Lord, making the infant the centerpiece of the scene, the mother says, I COMMEND HER TO THEE WITH HER SEED, TO PROTECT THEM FROM THE ACCURSED SATAN. Already the mighty seed of Mary is joined in thought with the emerging figure who exists for the purpose of nurturing that seed and bringing it to fruition.

When we leave the domain of Scripture, Christians and Muslims diverge widely in their interpretation of Mary, so widely that I have not chosen in this context to explore the avenues of rich development either of Mariology in Christian thought, or of the veneration of Mary in Islam. I shall keep to the Scriptural material in this paper for the most part.

My approach to the Scriptural data calls for two other preliminary remarks:

1) I am interested in the cross-referencing of the two religious traditions, to use a term of Kenneth Cragg.[2] The Scripture of one religion is not set forth as the standard beside which the other Scripture is placed, to see how it measures up. Instead, the two Books interact with each other, with cross-referencing in both directions. The Appendix to this paper shows the biblical verses in the first column, and the qur'anic verses in the second, but this arrangement is chronological only. It does not indicate judgment of priority in importance or in truthfulness.

2) Such an approach requires that we not think of Islam (coming later than Christianity) as "borrowing" from Christianity in its elaboration of the figure of Mary, but rather that we consider both Islam and Christianity as drawing upon a common store of information and inspiration, a fund of material that goes beyond either what the Bible says or what the Qur'an says about Mary.

Looking at the printed texts arranged in parallel columns in the Appendix, the qur'anic passages are taken from Arberry's translation and the biblical passages are from the Revised Standard Version. The following parallels may be noted:

(a) The first heading (see Appendix) is the "Family of Joseph" and the "Family of Mary," so we have a summary background of the legal parents of Jesus. In dealing with the family members of Mary and Joseph, serious difficulties have long been noted: Mary, as a member of the family of Imran (Qur'an 3:33-37), is called the sister of Aaron (Qur'an 19:28), suggesting a confusion of her identity with that of Miriam in the Hebrew Scriptures (Exodus 15:20). Joseph's father is named Jacob in Matthew's account but Heli in Luke 3:23. So exegetes made a tremendous effort to clear up these discrepancies or differences. However, efforts to clear up these problems are not entirely adequate, at least not to everyone's satisfaction. The names given may represent a symbolic approach to the family background of Mary and Joseph, rather than a strictly genealogical approach.

(b) Regarding the *dedication* of the infant Mary to God by her Mother, unnamed in the Qur'an, and named St. Anne in extra-biblical sources, this incident paves the way for the important stage in Mary's life, that is,

(c) Her miraculous *purification*. Christians depend on the extra-biblical sources for their information about this event. But in the Qur'an it is clearly said that the child will be protected from the accursed Satan. See Qur'an 3:42 for another mention of the purification.

(d) In the Bible Zechariah is not brought into direct touch with Mary, although he is an important figure, as the father of John the Baptist, in preparing the way for Jesus. On the other hand, the qur'anic story of Zechariah's *watching over the young Mary* and her testimony to the exuberant mercy of God (3:37) sets the tone for the lavish display of divine mercy soon to be described in the coming pivotal event of Mary's life, for Mary says, TRULY GOD PROVISIONS WHOMSOEVER HE WILL WITHOUT RECKONING.

(e) Without going into the details of the *announcement of Mary's conception*, we note the following parallels:

(f) *Withdrawal* of Mary from human society to a place apart from the world. In the Qur'an this occurs before the appearance of the angel, whereas in the Bible Mary goes to the hill country of Judah after the announcement of the angel.

(g) The *messenger* of God is Gabriel (Gospel), the divine Spirit in the form of a man (Qur'an), and a collective angelic announcement (Qur'an).

(h) The Bible records the *salutation* of the angel to Mary, but the Qur'an simply states that the messenger presented himself to her.

(i) Mary's surprise and troubled *state of mind* are noted in both the Qur'an and the Bible. In the Gospel, it simply states that she was troubled and perplexed. But the Qur'an shows her perplexity and her troubled state of mind in her prayerful seeking of refuge in God and her appeal to the messenger's integrity (19:18).

(j) The angel *reassures* Mary, and, in the same breath,

(k) gives the *promise* of a child. The elaboration of the promise, found in Qur'an 3:45, is packed with information about Jesus. Sura (Chapter) 3 of the Qur'an is a later revelation than Sura 19.

(l) Mary's *perplexity* on hearing the promise of a child focuses on her virginity: HOW CAN THIS BE, she says, SINCE I HAVE NO HUSBAND?

(m) *Reassurance* comes as the messenger in the Gospel describes the holy, divine, miraculous birth, and adds confirmation by telling about Elizabeth (the kinswoman of Mary), who has conceived a child in her old age. The qur'anic word emphasizes the sovereign creative power of God (corresponding to Luke 1:37). Luke says, FOR WITH GOD NOTHING WILL BE IMPOSSIBLE. The Qur'an says, GOD CREATES WHAT HE WILL. WHEN HE DECREES A THING, HE DOES BUT SAY LET IT BE, AND IT IS.

Two other qur'anic passages speak of the mysterious divine action resulting in the virgin birth. Here it is a question of the "how" of the creative act. In the previously cited text, Sura 3, God simply says BE, and it is, whereas in Suras 21 and 66 there is a certain elaboration upon this, a statement very mysterious indeed, but an approach at least to the "how" of this divine creative act. Take Sura 66:12, which is astonishing indeed. AND MARY, IMRAN'S DAUGHTER, WHO GUARDED HER VIRGINITY, SO WE BREATHED INTO HER OF OUR SPIRIT, AND SHE CONFIRMED THE WORDS OF HER LORD AND HIS BOOKS, AND BECAME ONE OF THE OBEDIENT.

Arberry's translation of this verse (see the Appendix) conceals the concrete meaning of the original Arabic. He translates the first part of the verse figuratively or idiomatically, AND MARY . . . GUARDED HER VIRGINITY; but the literal meaning of the Arabic brings the generative organs of the woman into the picture: WA MARYAMA IBNATA 'IMRAN ALLATI AHSANAT FARJAHA . . . (AND MARY, THE DAUGHTER OF IMRAN, WHO GUARDED HER VULVA . . .). According to Arberry, the second part of the verse says that God breathed into *her* of His spirit, but grammatically the Arabic seems to say that God breathed into *it* (i.e., her vulva): FA-NAFAKHNA FIHI MIN RUHINA. In this way divine power is said to have brought about pregnancy in Mary.

This striking figurative language in the Qur'an finds a parallel in the Gospel of Luke (1:35), where the angel says to the Virgin: THE HOLY SPIRIT WILL COME UPON YOU, AND THE POWER OF THE MOST HIGH WILL OVERSHADOW YOU; THEREFORE THE CHILD TO BE BORN WILL BE CALLED HOLY, THE SON OF GOD. The original Greek of this verse is as follows: PNEUMA HAGION EPELEUSETAI EPI SE, KAI DUNAMIS HUPSISTOU EPISKIASEI SOI. DIO KAI TO GENNOMENON HAGION KLETHESETAI HUIOS THEOU.

The divine spirit is the active force in both Scriptural statements. In Luke, the action is mysterious (COME UPON, OVERSHADOW) and less concrete than in the Qur'an. However, the result is the same in both cases: pregnancy in the virgin womb. And the Gospel goes on to specify further the outcome of this divine intervention in Mary's life: a HOLY child, the SON OF GOD.

The Qur'an is silent as to Mary's response to this reassurance, but the Bible enlarges on her faithful response and her overflowing joy as the realization dawns that she is the object of extraordinary divine favor (Luke 1:38, 46-55). So we have the beautiful song of Mary which Christians sing and recite constantly in their services of worship, MY SOUL MAGNIFIES THE LORD AND MY SPIRIT REJOICES IN GOD, MY SAVIOR, Mary's grateful response to the reassurance of the angel.

(n) Telling of the *birth of Jesus,* the Gospel describes its taking place in a semi-public setting, amid the crowds in Bethlehem, in a busy inn-yard, with an audience of shepherds not long after. In contrast, the Qur'an tells of an absolutely private birth in the desert: SHE CONCEIVED HIM AND WITHDREW WITH HIM TO A DISTANT PLACE, AND THE BIRTHPANGS SURPRISED HER BY THE TRUNK OF THE PALM-TREE.

(o) The Gospel discreetly notes the *people's lack of understanding* by giving Joseph's plan to divorce Mary when he found her pregnant. By contrast the Qur'an describes a sharp confrontation between Mary and her people, and a miraculous defense by the voice of the infant Jesus.

(p) The Scriptures are concerned to show how Mary was strengthened in her faith and also challenged after bearing her son. Only the Qur'an records her momentary wavering as she gives birth in the desert. And we have a combined witness or testimony of shepherds, wisemen, miraculously provided food and drink, an aged saint's inspired words, and a mysterious voice all joining to amaze and confound the humble virgin. Her response is to "ponder" these things in her heart (Gospel), and to vow a fast to God (Qur'an).

Mary has no title in the Scriptures of either Islam and Christianity. However, in two Suras of the Qur'an (19 and 21), the accounts of her life-transforming experiences are placed in a context of stories about the prophets. Therefore, there is justification for the statement, supported by many Muslims, that Mary was one of the prophets from God.

In what is said about Mary in Qur'an and Bible, we, who live in the aftermath of thirteen centuries of discussion, sense that we are only a step away from all of the stark and apparently irreducible divergence that exists between Islam and Christianity: the questions of the divine sonship of Jesus, of original sin, and of the incarnation. It has not been my purpose to develop the nature of this multiple divergence. Rather I have stressed the Scriptural figure of Mary that draws Muslims and Christians together. Perhaps in mutual contemplation of this holy woman, who with her child is A SIGN UNTO ALL BEINGS (Qur'an 21:91), we shall together learn to deal more adequately with our religious disagreements, and even better, perhaps we can take steps together, Muslims and Christians, to share that superlative quality of Mary, mirrored by her words in the Gospel, LET IT BE TO ME ACCORDING TO YOUR WORD" (Luke 1:38) and described in the Qur'an as SHE BECAME ONE OF THE OBEDIENT (66:12).

ENDNOTES

[1]A remark made regarding Mary in the Bible, by Catharina Halkes, "Mary and Women," *Concilium* (Oct., 1983):68.

[2]Kenneth Cragg, *The Christ and the Faiths* (Philadelphia, 1986).

APPENDIX

MARY, MOTHER OF JESUS, IN CHRISTIAN AND ISLAMIC TRADITION

BIBLE

(a) FAMILY OF JOSEPH

Mt. 1:1, 16
The book of the genealogy of Jesus Christ, the son of David, the son of Abraham. . .and Jacob father of Joseph the husband of Mary, of whom Jesus was born, who is called the Christ.

QUR'AN

(a) FAMILY OF MARY

3:33-37
God chose Adam and Noah
and the House of Abraham
and the House of Imran
above all beings, the
seed of one another;
God hears, and knows.

(b) (Mary's mother dedicates her to God)
When the wife of Imran
said 'Lord, I have vowed
to Thee, in dedication,
what is within my womb.
Receive Thou this from me;
Thou hearest, and knowest.'
And when she gave birth to her,
she said 'Lord, I have given
birth to her, a female.'
(And God knew very well
what she given birth to;
the male is not as the female.)
'And I have named her Mary,
and commend her to Thee
with her seed,

(c) (Purification of Mary)
to protect them
from the accursed Satan.'
Her Lord received the child
with gracious favour,
and by His goodness
she grew up comely,

(d) (Zachariah watches over Mary)
Zachariah taking
charge of her. Whenever
Zachariah went in to her
in the Sanctuary, he
found her provisioned.
'Mary,' he said,
'how comes this to thee?'
'From God,' she said.
Truly God provisions
whomsover He will
without reckoning.

(e) ANNOUNCEMENT OF CONCEPTION

Lk. 1:26-56
(g) In the sixth month the angel Gabriel was sent
from God to a city of Galilee named
Nazareth, to a virgin betrothed to a man
whose name was Joseph, of the house of
David; and the virgin's name was Mary.
(h) And he came to her and said, "Hail, O
favored one, the Lord is with you!" But
(i) she was greatly troubled at the saying
and considered in her mind what sort of
greeting this might be. And the angel
(j) said to her, "Do not be afraid, Mary, for
you have found favor with God. And
behold, you will conceive in your womb,
(k) and bear a son, and you shall call his
name Jesus.
He will be great, and will be called
the Son of the Most High; and the Lord
God will give to him the throne of his
father David, and he will reign over the
house of Jacob for ever; and of his
kingdom there will be no end." And Mary
(l) said to the angel, "How can this be,
since I have no husband?" And the angel
(m) said to her, "The Holy Spirit will come
upon you, and the power of the Most High
will overshadow you; therefore the child
to be born will be called holy, the Son
of God.
And behold, your kinswoman Elizabeth
in her old age has also conceived a son;
and this is the sixth month with her who
was called barren. For with God nothing
will be impossible." And Mary said,
"Behold I am the handmaid of the Lord;
let it be to me according to your word."
And the angel departed from her.
(f) In those days Mary arose and went with (f)
haste into the hill country, to a city of
Judah, and she entered the house of
Zechariah and greeted Elizabeth. And when
Elizabeth heard the greeting of Mary, the
babe leaped in her womb; and Elizabeth
was filled with the Holy Spirit and she
exclaimed with a loud cry, "Blessed are
you among women, and blessed is the fruit of
your womb! And why is this granted me,
that the mother of my Lord should come to
me? For behold, when the voice of your
greeting came to my ears, the babe in my womb
leaped for joy. And blessed is she

19:16-21
And mention in the Book Mary
(f) when she withdrew from her people
to an eastern place,
and she took a veil apart from them;
(g) then We sent unto her Our Spirit
that presented himself to her
(h) a man without fault.
She said, 'I take refuge in
the All-merciful from Thee!
If thou fearest God . . . .'
(j) He said, 'I am but a messenger
come from thy Lord, to give thee
(k) a boy most pure.'
(l) She said, 'How shall I have a son
whom no mortal has touched, neither
have I been unchaste?'
He said, 'Even so thy Lord has said:
"Easy is that for me; and that We
(m) may appoint him a sign unto men
and a mercy from Us; it is
a thing decreed."'

3:42-47
And when the angels said,
(g) 'Mary, God has chosen
thee, and purified
(c) thee; He has chosen
thee above all women.
Mary, be obedient to
thy Lord, prostrating
and bowing before Him.'
(That is of the tidings
of the Unseen, that We
reveal to thee; for thou
wast not with them, when
they were casting quills
which of them should have
charge of Mary; thou
wast not with them, when
they were disputing.)
When the angels said,
(k) 'Mary, God gives thee good
tidings of a Word from Him
whose name is Messiah,
Jesus, son of Mary;
high honoured shall he be
in this world and the next,
near stationed to God.
He shall speak to men
in the cradle, and of age,
and righteous he shall be.'

who believed that there would be a fulfillment of what was spoken to her from the Lord." And Mary said, "My soul magnifies the Lord, and my spirit rejoices in God my Savior, for he has regarded the low estate of his handmaiden. For behold, henceforth all generations will call me blessed; for he who is mighty and has done great things for me, and holy is his name. And his mercy is on those who fear him from generation to generation. He has shown strength with his arm, he has scattered the proud in the imagination of their hearts, he has put down the mighty from their thrones, and exalted those of low degree; he has filled the hungry with good things, and the rich he has sent empty away. He has helped his servant Israel, in remembrance of his mercy, as he spoke to our fathers, to Abraham and to his posterity forever." And Mary remained with her about three months, and returned to her home.

(l) 'Lord' said Mary,
'how shall I have a son
seeing no mortal has
touched me?' 'Even so,'
(m) God said, 'God
creates what He will.
When He decrees a thing
He does but say to it
"Be," and it is.

21:91
(m) And she who guarded her virginity,
so We breathed into her Our spirit
and appointed her and he son to be a
sign unto all beings.

66:12
(m) And Mary, Imran's daughter,
who guarded her virginity,
so We breathed into her of
Our Spirit, and she confirmed
the Words of her Lord and His
Books, and became one of
the obedient.

BIRTH OF JESUS

Lk. 2:4-7
(n) And Joseph also went up from Galilee, from the city of Nazareth, to Judea, to the city of David, which is called Bethlehem, because he was of the house and lineage of David, to be enrolled with Mary, his betrothed, who was with child. And while they were there, the time came for her to be delivered, And she gave birth to her first-born son and wrapped him in swaddling clothes, and laid him in a manger, because there was no place for them in the inn.

Mt. 1:18-25
Now the birth of Jesus Christ took place in this way. When his mother Mary had been betrothed to Joseph, before they came together she was found to be with child of the Holy Spirit;

19:22,23a
So she conceived him, and withdrew with him to a distant place. And the
(n) birthpangs surprised her by the trunk of the palm-tree.

(o) THE PEOPLE'S LACK OF UNDERSTANDING

and her husband Joseph, being a just man and unwilling to put her to shame, resolved to divorce her quietly. But as he considered this, behold, an angel of the Lord appeared to him in a dream, saying, "Joseph, son of David, do not fear to take Mary your wife, for that which is conceived in her is of the Holy Spirit; she will bear a son, and you shall call his name Jesus, for he will save his people from their sins." All this took place to fulfill what the Lord had spoken by the prophet: "Behold, a virgin shall conceive and bear a son, and his name shall be called Emmanuel" (which means, God with us). When Joseph woke from sleep, he did as the angel of the Lord commanded him; he took his wife, but knew her not until she had borne as son; and he called his name Jesus.

4:155,156
God sealed them . . . for their unbelief, and their uttering against Mary a mighty calumny, . . .

19:27-32
Then she brought the child to her folk
carrying him; and they said,
'Mary, thou hast surely committed
a monstrous thing!
Sister of Aaron, thy father was not
a wicked man, nor was thy mother
a woman unchaste.'
Mary pointed to the child then;
but they said, 'How shall we speak
to one who is still in the cradle,
a little child?'
He said, 'Lo, I am God's servant;
God has given me the Book, and
made me a Prophet.
Blessed He has made me, wherever
I may be; and He has enjoined me
to pray, and to give the alms, so
long as I live,
and likewise to cherish my mother.

(p) CONFIRMATION AND COMFORT FOR MARY

Lk. 2:16-19
And they (the shepherds) went with haste, and found Mary and Joseph, and the babe lying in a manger. And when they saw it they made known they saying which had been told them concerning the child; and all who heard it wondered at what the shepherds told them. But Mary kept all these things, pondering them in her heart.

Mt. 2:10-11
When they (the wisemen) saw the star, they rejoiced exceedingly with great joy; and going into the house they saw the child with Mary his mother, and they fell down and worshiped him. Then, opening their treasures, they offered him gifts, gold and frankincense and myrrh.

Lk. 2:33-35
And his father and his mother marveled at what was said about him; and Simeon

19: 23b-26
She said,
'Would I had died ere this, and become
a thing forgotten!"
But the one that was below her
called to her, 'Nay, do not sorrow;
see, the Lord has set below thee
a rivulet.
Shake also to thee the palm-trunk,
and there shall come tumbling upon thee
dates fresh and ripe.
East therefore, and drink, and be
comforted; and if thou shouldest see
any mortal,
say, "I have vowed to the All-merciful
a fast, and today I will not speak
to any man."

blessed them, and said to Mary his mother, "Behold, this child is set for the fall and rising of many in Israel, and for a sign that is spoken against (and a sword will pierce through your own soul also), that thoughts our of many hearts may be revealed."

SUGGESTIONS FOR FURTHER READING

Brown, Raymond E., et al. (eds.). *Mary in the New Testament*. Philadelphia and New York, 1978.

Courtois, V. *Mary in Islam*. Calcutta, 1954.

Kerr, David A. "Mary, Mother of Jesus, in the Islamic Tradition: A Theme for Christian-Muslim Dialogue." *Encounter* 155 (1989):3-17.

Parrinder, G. *Jesus in the Qur'an*. New York, 1977.

Schuon, Frithjof. *Dimensions of Islam*. London, 1970.

Wensinck, A. J., and Penelope Johnstone. "Maryam." *Encyclopaedia of Islam*. New ed. Leiden, 1991.

THE REV. DR. R. MARSTON SPEIGHT is Director of the Office on Christian-Muslim Relations of the National Council of Churches in the U.S., and a member of the adjunct faculty of Hartford Seminary. He received his Ph.D. in History of Religions from Hartford Seminary Foundation (1970), and his ordination in the United Methodist Church (1963).

JESUS IN THE QUR'AN: SOME SIMILARITIES AND DIFFERENCES WITH THE NEW TESTAMENT

Muzammil H. Siddiqi

Jesus is the common link between Islam and Christianity. Muslims believe in Jesus as they believe in Muhammad and other prophets of God. Prophet Muhammad is not the only prophet in Islam--he is only one of the many prophets of God. Before him came many prophets who preached the same message of submission to God, that is, Islam. The uniqueness of Muhammad, according to Muslim beliefs, is that he is the final prophet and messenger of God. Islam does not recognize any prophet after Muhammad.

Jesus is called *'Isa* in the Qur'an. He is also known as *al-Masih* (the Christ) and *Ibn Maryam* (Son of Mary). He has many other beautiful names and titles in the Qur'an. He is a highly respected religious figure. Outside the Christian church, there is no religious community that has given Jesus as much honor, respect, esteem and love as Muslims have done.

I. The Qur'an and Bible as Sources for the Life of Jesus

The Qur'an and the New Testament are the two most important sacred texts that have spoken about Jesus. The nature of these two texts is, however, quite different. The central theme of the Qur'an is not Jesus, but God. The Qur'an mentions Jesus as one among the many great prophets of God. The Qur'an talks about God on every page and tells us about what He has done and continues to do for humankind, and what He wants from them. God's prophets came for this very purpose. They came to remind people about their relation with God and His creation. For the authors of the New Testament, Jesus is the main figure. He is the center and the focus of the New Testament story. They talk about his life, death and resurrection. They focus on his teachings, his message, and the response of his contemporaries to him.

It is comparatively easy to present the Christology of the Qur'an. The Qur'an is one book, coming from one source. It was presented, memorized, and preserved within the life of Prophet Muhammad and shortly thereafter. Muslims believe that the Qur'an is the *ipsissima verba* of God. It is, literally, *the* word of God. God revealed the Qur'an to Prophet Muhammad over a period of twenty-three years of his prophetic career. For Muslims, it contains the most authoritative truth about all matters of importance. The New Testament is a collection of twenty-seven books, written by at least twelve different authors between 50 and 200 years after Jesus. These authors wrote in a language that Jesus never spoke and, probably, did not even know. These writers had no personal acquaintance with Jesus, nor did they ever meet him. It is for this reason that New Testament lacks a personal and physical description of Jesus. Basic biographical information about Jesus is very minimal in the New Testament. Many Christians hold that the authors of the New Testament were inspired by the Holy Spirit. However, more critical readers of these texts, both among Catholics and Protestants, have found many inconsistencies. Many of them are increasingly inclined to believe that, instead of representing the Holy Spirit, these authors were representing a variety of views and theologies that were held by different individuals and groups in the Greco-Roman world in the early centers of Christianity. Thus, the task of the discovery of "historical Jesus" and the reconstruction of a uniform New Testament Christology is extremely difficult, if not impossible.

Some Christians argue that the New Testament came centuries earlier than the Qur'an and is, chronologically, closer to the time of Jesus.[1] Thus, from a historical point of view, they claim, it is a more reliable source about Jesus than the Qur'an. Therefore, they contend that wherever the Qur'an and the New Testament differ concerning Jesus, such as on the question of crucifixion, the New Testament should be given preference to the Qur'an, because of its historical antecedence. However, New Testament documents do not represent the earliest information about Jesus. The four Canonical Gospels represent only a fraction of what was written about Jesus in early centuries. They represent only the Nicene orthodoxy as it emerged in the fourth century after many debates and theological controversies. For those reasons, some Christian scholars are beginning to recognize that the Qur'an, which comes later in history, contains a tradition about Jesus that may precede even the Canonical tradition.

II. Similarities in the Qur'an and the New Testament about Jesus

Jesus is the son of Mary. The Qur'an often refers to him as *Ibn Maryam* (a total of twenty-two times, see 2:87; 2:253 and others). Some questions have been raised whether the Arabic name *'Isa* actually refers to Jesus, or to a different person. The Arabic word *'Isa* is probably just a phonetic variant on the Syriac *Yeshu'a*. Furthermore, 'Isa's identity as Jesus is assured because of his mother, Mary.

The Qur'an also accepts Jesus' virgin birth (see 3:45-47 and 19:16-36). It speaks about it in very strong terms. "How can I have a child when no male has touched me?" Mary said to the angel who announced to her the birth of a child (see 3:47; 19:20 and also 66:12). Jesus is called *Kalimatuhu* (3:45, "His Word") and *Ruh minhu* (4:71, "A spirit from Him"). Both titles are associated with his miraculous birth. In the Qur'an they bear no incarnational connotation. *The Qur'an does not use Kalimah* in the same sense as *Logos* in the Gospel of John. Similarly, *Ruh* (spirit) is distinct from *Hayat* (life). According to the Qur'an, Jesus was created miraculously through the intervention of the Spirit from God (generally interpreted as sending the angel Gabriel to Mary to give her the news of his miraculous birth). The Qur'an clearly rejects the idea of God's incarnating Himself or begetting a son (see 2:116; 10:68; 17:111; 19:88, and others). The Qur'an never calls Jesus "the son of God."

The Qur'an gives Jesus many other titles of honor and respect. Some of these titles are similar to those he has in the New Testament. He is often called *al-Masih* ("The Christ"; this title occur about eleven times, see 3:45, 4:157, 171, 172, and others). The Qur'an does not give this title to anyone other than Jesus. He is the only recipient of this title. The Qur'an, however, does not seem to give this title any eschatological meaning. It is an earthly title of Jesus. It is, perhaps, used in its most obvious meaning "The annointed person" or "The blessed person"; Jesus is also called *Mubarak* ("A blessed person"; see 19:31).

Jesus is, of course, a prominent messenger of God. So the Qur'an calls him *Rasul Allah* ("Messenger of Allah"; see 4:157, 171). He is also a "Servant of God" (*'Abd*; see 43:59, 4:172). He is "honorable in this world and in the hereafter" (*wajihan fi al-dunya wa al-akhirah*, 3:45) and he is one of those "brought closer to God" (*min al-muqarrabin*, 3:45). He is "a sign" (*aya*, 19:21) and "a mercy" (*rahma*, 19:21) from God.

The Qur'an says that Jesus performed many miracles. The Qur'an uses the word *"bi-idhni"* ("by My permission"; this expression occurs four times in 5:110, with every type of miracle) to indicate that Jesus was only an agent and whatever he did was not by his own will or power but by the power and permission of God alone.

The message of Jesus, the Qur'an says, was that of commitment to God. He used to say, GOD IS MY LORD AND YOUR LORD, SO WORSHIP HIM (19:36). He taught righteousness and wisdom (3:49; 5:112-120). He was the messenger of truth and love.

The Qur'an mentions the difficulties that Jesus encountered in performing his mission and presenting his message. He was denied, rejected, accused, and abused (see 3:52; 4:156). He asked his followers to support him and assist him (3:52; 61:14). But after this the New Testament and the Qur'an part company. According to the New Testament Jesus was finally crucified and put to death. But the Qur'an rejects this assertion. THEY KILLED HIM NOT, NOR DID THEY CRUCIFY HIM . . . (4:57). According to the Qur'an neither the crucifixion of Jesus took place, nor his death at the hands of his enemies. The circumstances, however, created some confusion/illusion in people's minds about the end of his earthly life. The Qur'an removes this confusion by saying that God lifted Jesus toward Him. AND THOSE WHO DIFFER IN THIS MATTER THEY ARE IN DOUBT. THEY HAVE NO SURE KNOWLEDGE, EXCEPT CONJECTURE TO FOLLOW. SURELY THEY KILLED HIM NOT (4:157).

III. Differences between the Qur'an and New Testament Concerning Jesus

Unlike the New Testament, the Qur'an emphasizes that Jesus came to affirm the unity of God. He did not teach the Trinity. He asked his followers to worship God alone, Who is his Lord and their Lord (3:51; 19:36; 43:64). The Qur'an asks Christians to shun the doctrine of the Trinity. BELIEVE IN ALLAH AND HIS MESSENGERS AND DO NOT SAY, 'TRINITY,' DESIST, IT WILL BE BETTER FOR YOU (4:171). It also says, SURELY THE UNBELIEVERS ARE THOSE WHO SAY, 'GOD IS THE THIRD OF THE THREE,' FOR THERE IS NO GOD EXCEPT ONE GOD . . . (5:73). However, the Persons of the Trinity are not identified in the Qur'an. Whatever they may be, the concept itself is unacceptable and is contrary to the message of Jesus.

On the Day of Judgement, the Qur'an says, God will ask Jesus, O JESUS, SON OF MARY, DID YOU SAY TO THE PEOPLE, 'WORSHIP ME AND MY MOTHER AS TWO GODS OTHER THAN ALLAH'? Jesus will answer, 'GLORY TO YOU, NEVER I COULD SAY WHAT HAVE NO RIGHT TO SAY.' HAD I SAID SUCH A THING YOU WOULD HAVE SURELY KNOWN IT. YOU KNOW WHAT IS IN MY HEART, THOUGH I DO NOT KNOW WHAT IS IN YOURS.

FOR YOU KNOW IN FULL ALL THAT IS HIDDEN (5:116). Based on this verse some Christian scholars have suggested that according to the Qur'an the Trinity consists of "Father, Mother, and Son" and not "Father, Son, and Holy Spirit."[2] Since the former is not generally held Christian view of the Trinity, these scholars argue that either the Qur'an has mistaken the Trinity or it has criticized the wrong notion of the Trinity, but not the orthodox notion of the Trinity. Actually, in 5:116 there is no discussion of the Trinity. It discusses the false notion of the divinity of Jesus and Mary that was held by some Christians. From the qur'anic perspective, it does not make any difference whether the Trinity is "Father, Son, and Holy Spirit" or "Father, Mother, and Son." Every notion of the Trinity of God is unacceptable to the Qur'an, regardless of its interpretation.

The Qur'an also stresses the fact that Jesus never claimed himself to be "God," "Son of God," "Lord," "God incarnate," or co-equal or co-substantial with God. In the Gospels, too, Jesus is not told to have made use of these titles for himself. More than seventy times he calls himself "son of man" and only twice "son of God," but according to new critical studies of the Gospels these are not most probably his own words.[3] Also many critical New Testament Scholars have pointed out that in Aramaic or Hebrew the expression "son of God" means only "the one who is blessed by God" and nothing else.[4]

The Qur'an does not say that Jesus denied the importance of Mosaic law or rejected it or asked his followers not to follow it. Jesus, according to the Qur'an, was very much like the Israelite prophets. He did not introduce any new law, but he was sent to confirm the previous laws that were given to Moses.

As mentioned earlier in this paper, the Qur'an has denied that Jesus was killed or crucified. Along with this, all the concomitant notions of Original Sin, redemption and ransom do not find any place in qur'anic theology or in its discussion about Jesus.

IV. Dialogue between Islam and Christianity

Dialogue between Muslims and Christians is very important. We have many issues to discuss that are at the core of our two traditions. Instead of shying away from discussion, we should talk about these issues in an atmoshpere of friendship and frankness. After all, we are all members of one Abrahamic family that needs reconciliation. We come to dialogue at least to have a better understanding of each other.

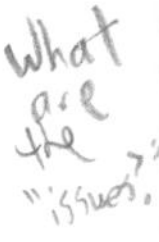

May the Peace and Blessings of God be with us all in this important undertaking.

APPENDIX

The following are the main quotations of the Holy Qur'an concerning Mary and Jesus:

Al-i-Imran 35-36) Behold! a woman of Imran said: 'O my Lord! I do dedicate (3: unto Thee what is in my womb for Thy special service; so accept this of me; for Thou hearest and knowest all things.' When she was delivered she said: 'O my Lord! behold! I am delivered of a female child!' - And Allah knew best what she brought forth - 'And nowise is the male like the female. I have named her Mary, and I commend her and her offspring to Thy protection from the Evil One, the Rejected.'

(3:37) Right graciously did her Lord accept her; He made her grow in purity and beauty; to the care of Zakariyya was she assigned. Every time that he entered (her) chamber to see her, he found her supplied with sustenance. He said: 'O Mary! Whence (comes) this to you?' She said: 'From Allah; for Allah provides sustenance to whom He pleases without measure.'

(3:42-43) Behold! the angels said: 'O Mary! Allah hath chosen thee and purified thee - chosen thee above the women of all nations. O Mary! worship thy Lord devoutly; prostrate thyself, and bow down (in prayer) with those who bow down.'

(3:44) This part of the tidings of the things unseen, which We reveal unto thee (O messenger!) by inspiration. Thou wast not with them when they cast lots with arrows, as to which of them should be charged with the care of Mary; nor wast thou with them when they disputed (the point).

Maryam (19:16-19) Relate in the Book (the story of) Mary, when she withdrew from her family to a place in the East. She placed a screen (to screen herself) from them; then We sent to her our angel, and he appeared before her as a man in all respects. She said: 'I seek refuge from thee to (Allah) Most Gracious; (come not near) if thou dost fear Allah.' He said: 'Nay, I am only a messenger from the Lord, (to announce) to thee the gift of a son endowed with purity.'

Al-i-Imran (3:45-46) Behold! the angels said: 'O Mary! Allah giveth thee glad tidings of a word from Him; his name will be Christ Jesus, the son of Mary, held in honour in this world and the hereafter and of (the company of) those nearest to Allah. He shall speak to the people in childhood and in maturity, and he shall be (of the company) of the righteous.'

(3:47) She said: 'O my Lord! How shall I have a son when no man hath touched me?' He said: 'Even so: Allah createth what He willeth; when He hath decreed a plan, He but saith to it "Be," and it is!'

(3:48-51) 'And Allah will teach him the Book and Wisdom, the Law and the Gospel, and (appoint him) a messenger to the children of Israel (with this message): "I have come to you, with a sign from your Lord, in that I make for you out of clay, as it were, the figure of a bird, and breathe into it, and it becomes a bird by Allah's leave; and I heal those born blind, and the lepers, and I quicken the dead, by Allah's leave; and I declare to you what ye eat, and what ye store in your houses. Surely therein is a sign for you if ye did believe. (I have come to you) to attest the Law which was before me, and to make lawful to you part of what was (before) forbidden to you; I have come to you with a sign from your Lord; so fear Allah and obey me. It is Allah Who is my Lord and your Lord; then worship Him. This is a way that is straight."'

Maryam (19:22-23) So she conceived him, and she retired with him to a remote place. And the pains of childbirth drove her to the trunk of a palm-tree; she cried (in her anguish): 'Ah! would that I had died before this! Would that I had been a thing forgotten and out of sight!'

(19:24-26) But (a voice) cried to her from beneath the (palm-tree): 'Grieve not! for thy Lord hath provided a rivulet beneath thee; and shake towards thyself the trunk of the palm-tree; it will let fall fresh ripe dates upon thee. So eat and drink and cool (thine) eye. And if thou dost see any man, say "I have vowed a fast to (Allah) Most Gracious, and this day will I enter into no talk with any human being."'

(19:27-29) At length she brought the (babe) to her people, carrying him (in her arms). They said: 'O Mary! Truly an amazing thing hast thou brought! O sister of Aaron! Thy father was not a man of evil, nor thy mother a woman unchaste!' But she pointed to the babe. They said: 'How can we talk to one who is a child in the cradle?'

(19:30-34) He said: 'I am indeed a servant of Allah; He hath given me revelation and made me a prophet; and He hath made me blessed wheresoever I be, and hath enjoined on me prayer and charity as long as I live; (He) hath made me kind to my mother, and not overbearing or miserable; so peace is on me the day I was born, the day that I die, and the day that I shall be raised up to life (again)!' Such (was) Jesus the son of Mary; (it is) a statement of truth, about which they (vainly) dispute.

Baqara (2:97) We gave Jesus the son of Mary clear (signs) and strengthened him with the holy spirit.

Al-i-Imran (3:52-54) When Jesus found unbelief on their part he said: 'Who will be my helpers to (the work of) Allah?' Said the disciples: 'We are Allah's helpers; we believe in Allah, and do thou bear witness that we are Muslims. Our Lord! we believe in what Thou hast revealed, and we follow the messenger; then write us down among those who bear witness.' And (then unbelievers) plotted and planned, and Allah too planned, and the best of planners is Allah.

(3:55-58) Behold! Allah said: 'O Jesus! I will take thee and lift thee to Myself and clear thee (of the falsehood) of those who blaspheme; I will make those who follow thee superior to those who reject faith, to the Day of Resurrection; then shall ye dispute. As to those who reject faith, I will punish them with terrible agony in this world and in the Hereafter, nor will they have anyone to help. As to those who believe and work righteousness, Allah will pay them (in full) their reward; but Allah loveth not those who do wrong. This is what We rehearse unto thee of the signs and the message of wisdom.'

(3:59) The similitude of Jesus before Allah is as that of Adam; He created him from dust, then said to him: 'Be,' and he was.

Ma'ida (5:112-116) Behold! the disciples said: 'O Jesus the son of Mary! Can thy Lord send down to us a table set (with viands) from heaven?' Said Jesus: 'Fear Allah, if ye have faith.' They said: 'We only wish to eat thereof and satisfy our hearts, and to know that thou hast indeed told us the truth; and that we ourselves may be witnesses to the miracle.'

(5:117-118) Said Jesus, the son of Mary: 'O Allah our Lord! Send us from heaven a table set (with viands), that there may be for us--for the first and the last of us--a solemn festival and a sign from Thee; and provide for our sustenance, for Thou art the best sustainer (of our needs).' Allah said: 'I will send it down to you; but if any of you after that resisteth faith, I will punish him with a penalty such as I have not inflicted on anyone among all the peoples.'

(5:49-50) We sent Jesus the son of Mary, confirming the Law that had come before him; We sent him the Gospel; therein was guidance and light, and confirmation of the Law that had come before him; a guidance and an admonition to those who fear Allah. Let the people of the Gospel judge by what Allah hath revealed therein. If any do fail to judge by (the light of) what Allah hath revealed, they are (no better than) those who rebel.

Saff (61:6) And remember, Jesus, the son of Mary, said: 'O Children of Israel! I am the messenger of Allah (sent) to you confirming the Law (which came) before me, and giving glad tidings of a messenger to come after me, whose name shall be Ahmad.' But when he came to them with clear sign, they said, 'This is evident sorcery!'

Nisa' (4:156-158) (They--Jews--have incurred divine displeasure) that they uttered against Mary a grave false charge; that they said (in boast), 'We killed Christ Jesus the son of Mary, the messenger of Allah;' but they killed him not, nor crucified him, so it was made to appear to them, and those who differ therein are full of doubts, with no (certain) knowledge, but only conjecture to follow, for a survey they killed him not;--nay, Allah raised him up unto Himself; and Allah is Exalted in Power, Wise.

(4:159) And there is none of the People of the Book but must believe in him before his death; and on the Day of Judgement he will be a witness against them.

Zukhruf (43:59) He was no more than a servant; We granted our favour to him, and We made him an example to the Children of Israel.

(43:61) And (Jesus) shall be a sign (for the coming of) the Hour (of Judgement).

Tahrim (66:12) (Allah sets forth, as an example of those who believe) Mary, the daughter of Imran, who guarded her chastity; and We breathed into her (body) of our spirit; and she testified on the truth of the words of her Lord and of His revelations, and was one of the devout (servants).

Ma'ida (5:112-114) One day will Allah gather the messengers together, and ask: 'What was the response ye received (from men to your teaching)?' They will say: 'We have no knowledge; it is Thou Who knowest in full all that is hidden.' Then will Allah say: 'O Jesus the son of Mary! Recount My favour to thee and to thy mother. Behold! I strengthened thee with the holy spirit, so that thou didst speak to the people in childhood and in maturity. Behold! I taught thee the Book and Wisdom, the Law and the Gospel. And behold! thou makest out of clay, as it were, the figure of a bird, by My leave, and thou breathest into it, and it becometh a bird by My leave, and thou healest those born blind, and the lepers by My leave. And behold!

Thou bringest forth the dead by My leave. And behold! I did restrain the Children of Israel from (violence to) thee when thou didst show them the clear signs, and the unbelievers among them said: "This is nothing but evident magic." And behold! I inspired the disciples to have faith in Me and My messenger. They said: "We have faith, and do thou bear witness that we bow to Allah as Muslims."'

(5:119-121) And behold! Allah will say: 'O Jesus the son of Mary! Didst thou say unto men, "Worship me and my mother as gods in derogation of Allah"?' He will say: 'Glory to Thee! Never could I say what I had no right (to say). Had I said such a thing, Thou wouldst indeed have known it. Thou knowest what is in my heart, though I know not what is in Thine. For thou knowest in full all that is hidden. Never said I to them aught except what Thou didst command me to say, to wit, "Worship Allah, my Lord and your Lord"; and I was a witness over them whilst I dwelt among them; and Thou art a witness to all things. If Thou dost punish them, they are Thy servants; if Thou dost forgive them, Thou are the exalted, the Wise.'

(5:122) Allah will say: 'This is a day on which the truthful will profit from their truth; theirs are Gardens, with rivers flowing beneath, their eternal home; Allah well-pleased with them, and they with Allah. That is the great Salvation (the fulfillment of all desires).

ENDNOTES

[1]These and similar arguments are often made by Christian missionaries and polemicists in their debates with Muslims. See a study of this in Ahmad Shafaat, *Missionary Christianity and Islam*, part I, *The Question of Authenticity and Authority of the Bible* (Montreal: 1982). See also a recent work by Neal Robinson, *Christ in Islam and Christianity* (New York: 1991), especially chapter 2.

[2]"The question how Muhammad had come to conceive of Maryam as one of the persons of the Trinity has often been asked." See A. J. Wensinck, "Maryam" in *Shorter Encyclopaedia of Islam* (Leiden: 1974), 327-30.

[3]"In Roman Catholic seminaries, for example, it is now common teaching that Jesus of Nazarath did not assert any of the divine or messianic claims the Gospels attribute to him and that he died without believing he was Christ or the Son of God, not to mention the founder of a new religion." Thomas Sheehan, "Revolution in the Church" in *New York Review* (June 14, 1984). According to Hasting, "Whether Jesus used it (the expression 'Son of God') of Himself is doubtful." *Dictionary of the Bible* (rev. ed.; New York: 1963), 143.

Joseph Fitzmeyer, a leading biblical scholar in his *A Christological Catechism* asks, Did Jesus claim to be God? He answers, "the Gospels have not so presented that claim . . . . It is impossible to imagine how such a statement would have been understood." Quoted by Cullen Murphy in "Who Do Men Say That I Am?" in *The Atlantic Monthly* (December 1986):39.

[4]See James L. Price, *Interpreting the New Testament* (New York: 1961), 297. "He (Jesus) is not often represented as speaking of "the Son" in an absolute sense, and scholars often

question the genuineness of the passages where he is said to do so," said S. E. Johnson in "Son of God" in *The Interpreter's Dictionary of the Bible* (New York: 1962), 4:411.

SUGGESTIONS FOR FURTHER READING

See the Commentary on the above verses by 'Abdullah Yusuf 'Ali, *The Holy Qur'an: Text, Translation and Commentary* (many editions). Brattleboro, VT, 1989.

'Ata-ur-Rahman, Muhammad. *Jesus, Prophet of Islam*. Brooklyn, NY, 1977.

Parrinder, Geoffrey. *Jesus in the Qur'an*. New York, 1977.

Robinson, Neal. *Christ in Islam and Christianity*. New York, 1991.

MUZAMMIL H. SIDDIQI is Director of the Islamic Society of Orange County, California. He received his Ph.D. in Comparative Religion from Harvard University (1978). He is a graduate of the Islamic University of Medina (Saudi Arabia) and the Indian Islamic Seminary, Nadwatul 'Ulama in Lucknow.

PART II

HISTORY: INTERACTION AND PARALLEL DEVELOPMENT

HISTORICAL PERSPECTIVES ON JEWISH-MUSLIM RELATIONS

Marilyn Robinson Waldman

The main purpose of this essay is to show that Jewish-Muslim relationships have a history, and that Jews and Muslims in the United States are part of that history. To say that relationships have a history is to say that they have changed and are still changing. Indeed, Jews and Muslims have interacted with each other in many different places and situations for more than a millennium, and their historical experiences suggest that they are fully capable of adapting to the unprecedented circumstances in which they find themselves in the United States today. In fact, it is more important than ever to recognize the openness of history, and the variety of ways in which groups are capable of perceiving and relating to each other, regardless of any dark moments in their past.

Two personal experiences have taught me just how flexible and how complicated people's conceptions of religious identities can be. The first occurred after one of my lectures at a church in Columbus, when a woman came up and asked a question unprecedented in all my twenty years of teaching and lecturing: "Don't you consider the Muslims to be Gentiles?" I replied, "No, that never occurred to me." She protested, "But my mother brought me up to believe that the world is divided into two groups--Jews and Gentiles--and if you are not one, you are the other, and that makes Muslims, Gentiles."

The second experience arose from attending a lecture by an anthropologist who had worked in the Iranian town of Yazd, which has a very old Jewish community. The Jews of Yazd, like the woman at my lecture, have also divided the world into Goyim (Gentiles) and Galutim (peoples of the Diaspora). In their view, the Galutim include not only themselves, but also the Zoroastrians, the Armenian Christians, and the Sunni Muslims; the Gentiles consist simply of the Shi'i Muslims. To them, "Gentile" refers to any group that predominates or is in power; "Galutim," to anyone who is disenfranchised and out of power.

Jewish-Muslim relations have been as variable and complex as these two stories would suggest, and they have also been very extensive. In his editor's introduction to a volume of essays on Islamic-Judaic interactions, William Brinner makes the following observation:

> It is becoming increasingly clear that these two religions, Judaism and Islam, have interacted on a number of levels--from that of folklore and folk religion to the realms of theological and philosophical speculation. It is also becoming more apparent that for a variety of reasons, this interaction was probably more profound than that which existed between Islam and Christianity.[1]

If that is so, why has Jewish-Muslim interaction, not to mention Jewish-Christian interaction, received relatively little scholarly attention? First, until recently, these three religions have normally been studied by specialists in different fields, so opportunities to study their interaction have been limited and professionally unrewarding. Second, since most professional historians are themselves "western" and study "the west," they have generally defined Judaism and Christianity as "western" and Islam as "eastern." Thus, they have tended to overlook the fact that Judaism, Christianity, along with Islam, originated in "the east," and that all three continued to interact there long after some of the Jews and Christians had moved "west." Recent scholarship has begun to correct that oversight, and in this brief essay I summarize some of the major lessons it is teaching us about the history of Jewish-Muslim interaction.

Before attempting to learn those lessons, it is important to remember that Muslims and Jews have most often lived together in societies with very different social expectations from our own. The institutionalized equality of all human beings was virtually unknown anywhere in the world before modern times, so belonging to a religion other than that of the ruler often brought subordinate status of some sort. The assigning of lower status to non-dominant religions seems to have been a common pre-modern habit, not just in the Middle East, where Islam developed, but in Europe as well. We have only to look to the Protestant Reformation for an example of the distribution of subject peoples into religious communities with different statuses: if a ruler became Catholic, the Protestants suffered, and if a ruler became Protestant, the Catholics suffered.

An amusing apocryphal story well illustrates the trials of subordinate religious communities in medieval Europe. A bishop decided that the Jews in his town had to go. In the face of protest from the Jewish community, the bishop agreed to let them stay if one of them could defeat him in a public non-verbal duel of wits. Naturally, no Jew was quick to volunteer, but finally a poor tailor named Mentl reluctantly agreed.

The bishop arrived dressed in magnificent regalia and accompanied by a large entourage; the tailor came alone in his work clothes. The bishop drew a large circle, and the tailor stomped furiously on the ground. The bishop began to look a little nervous, but continued. He held up three fingers and Mentl held up one. The bishop began to sweat and seemed very nervous as he took the bread and the wine from under his garments and swallowed them, at which point Mentl took an apple out of his pocket and bit into it. The bishop threw up his hands and said, "That's it. The Jews can stay."

That afternoon, the bishop's followers asked what had happened, and he answered, "I drew a circle to remind us God is everywhere, but the Jew stomped on the ground to remind us that God is not in Hell. I held up three fingers to remind us of the Trinity, but he held up one to remind us of the oneness of God that it represents. I took out the bread and the wine to remind us of the sacrifice of our Lord, but he took out an apple to remind us of the sin that made it all necessary."

Across town, Mentl's friends asked him what had happened. "Well, he made this big circle to show us he wanted us outside the city walls, but I stomped on the ground to say, 'No way.' He held up three fingers to say he would give us three days to clear out, but I held up one to tell him not one of us is moving. And then when he took out his lunch, I took out mine."

This type of structure--subordinate religious communities under the power of a dominant ruler and his religion--was characteristic of the Roman and Sasanian empires, the pre-Islamic rulers of the areas that first came under Muslim rule. In many of the areas into which Arab-Muslims began to migrate the mid-seventh century of the Common Era (CE), religious communities were already functioning as separate bodies joined together primarily by their allegiance to a common ruler. Furthermore, rulers were already using the religious community as an important vehicle for social and political management, and for assigning social status, long before the emergence of the first Muslim empire.

The new Muslim rulers appear to have appropriated this social structure (though not right away) and institutionalized it in the form of *ahl al-dhimma*, or *dhimmis*, protected scriptural communities who had a subordinate legal status but lived largely under their own rules. Since most of the Muslim-ruled lands probably did not become majority Muslim until about 875, two hundred and fifty years after the beginning of the conquest, the early Muslim community was itself a minority in the lands over which it ruled. The subject majority was composed of Jews, Christians, and Zoroastrians.

So the hegemony of the Muslims had ironic effects. It eventually resulted in the conversion of some Jews and of most Christians and

Zoroastrians; but it protected from each other those who retained their religious affiliations, and even allowed them a degree of consolidation and renewal. The great scholar of Jewish-Muslim interaction, perhaps the greatest of our century, Shlomo Dov Goitein, once remarked that the establishment of Muslim hegemony revitalized and possibly saved medieval Judaism from extinction.

The relationships between Jews and Muslims living under this kind of socio-political structure have naturally not been ideal by today's American standards, which assume a very different structure. At best the structure in which the Muslims and Jews found themselves sometimes promoted, to be sure, tensions and unequal relationships. At worst, Jews experienced discrimination and persecution that violated Muslim ideals as well.

On the other hand, social mobility, intercommunal contact, and cultural freedom seem to have been far greater for a religious minority in the Muslim-ruled lands than in Christendom, and Jews benefited from that as much as any subject group. We have, for example, as many critiques of Islam by the Jewish scholar Maimonides (1135-1204 CE) as we have critiques of Judaism by any single Muslim scholar. So regardless of the imperfect political and social record, members of the two traditions have managed during the last fourteen centuries to influence each other in unpredictable and unexpected ways.

I want to illustrate that changeable pattern of mutual influence with brief sketches of four different situations: the community of Muhammad (622-632 CE), the early 'Abbasid empire (especially mid-eighth to mid-tenth century), al-Andalus ("Moorish Spain," especially the tenth to the thirteenth century); and the Ottoman Empire (fifteenth to twentieth century).

I. The Community of Muhammad

It is all too well known that the prophet Muhammad's relationships with the Jews of Arabia were often tense and sometimes even violent. The conflicts between Muhammad and his followers (Muslims) on the one hand and the Jews on the other are referred to not only in the Qur'an (the revelations of God as spoken by Muhammad), but also in early Muslim historical sources. Yet the Qur'an also reveres such figures as Abraham and Moses as legitimate prophets, and prescribes for Muslims certain requirements (e.g., multiple daily prayer) and taboos (e.g., against eating pork) that were shared by Jews.

In fact, then, Muhammad's relations with Jews were ambivalent. At the beginning of his prophethood, Muhammad appears to have thought of himself as a reformer within the Jewish (and Christian) tradition. As such, he expected Jews (and Christians) to recognize him and follow his lead. Some probably did; others resisted and even worked against the success and survival of his fledgling community. As a result, Muhammad began to think of himself as the proclaimer of a pure and "generic" surrender to God (Islam) that Jews (and Christians) had turned into their own "name-brand" religions over time. However, even after making that shift in emphasis, Muhammad offered Jews and Christians, as peoples who each had a Book from God, protection in return for submission to the political hegemony of the Muslim community.

The history I have just sketched is clear enough, but unfortunately we do not yet have a clear enough picture of Arabian "Jews" to understand it very well. Certainly, we must be very careful about using the Qur'an to explain relations between Jews and Muslims in our own time. In fact, the Qur'an uses two relevant labels--"Yahud" and "Banu Isra'il," so we cannot even know whether it is referring to a single people or group. Furthermore, individuals bearing those labels could belong to tribes of their own, or be mixed in the same tribe with members of other communities. Such individuals spoke Arabic, like the first Muslims, and may have been indistinguishable from other Arabic-speakers except in matters of personal habit and ritual practice. Finally, Muhammad's conflicts with them may have arisen more from their lack of support for the economic and political expansion of his community than from disagreements over faith and belief. Whatever the relationship between Arabian "Jews" and the first Muslims really was, many Jews outside of Arabia soon came under the rule of Muslims as *dhimmi*s. When, by 640, Muslim rulers had gained control over all of what we now call the Middle East, their relationships with the Jews of that region were of a different nature.

II. The Early 'Abbasid Empire

From the origins of the 'Abbasid dynasty in 750 to the tenth century, Jewish-Muslim interaction was particularly intense and the impact of Jews on Muslims particularly strong. During this period some Jews were becoming Muslims; some of the Jews who became Muslims, or their descendants, also became scholars of Islam; and Jews who did not become Muslim could still play a role in the development of the ideas and institutions of the Muslims. Marshall Hodgson, one of the most creative American scholars of Islamic history and civilization, even invented a new adjective, "Islamicate," to describe the participation of so many non-Muslims in the civilization that was inspired by the spread of Muslim rule and the Islamic faith.

Eventually Muslims came to think and act more "Islamically," and to view themselves as having superceded Jewish understanding of material in the Qur'an that was common to both traditions. Nevertheless, Jewish lore filtered into Islamic lore, particularly by means of a genre called "qisas al-anbiya'" (stories of the prophets), which reworked Jewish tradition to provide Islamic accounts of prophetic figures who are common to Jews and Muslims. Before long, all sorts of Muslims had absorbed and begun to use these shared materials. For example, the eleventh-century Persian author Bayhaqi, in the course of his narrative of Iranian history, illustrated the trait of compassion by recalling an occasion on which Moses took the time to return a lost lamb to its mother before continuing on his journey.[2] The story does not appear in the Torah or in the Qur'an, but does appear in Midrashic lore.

We also know that many Muslim scholars in the early 'Abbasid period specialized in the study of Jewish sectarianism. Since the Muslim taxation system made distinctions for various religious affiliations, Muslim rulers needed to know who could be considered Jews and who not. However, the 'Abbasids' Jewish subjects and their leaders often could not or would not tell or agree, so Muslim scholars made a point of finding out on their own. As a result, we know much of what we know about certain "Jewish" movements only through the accounts of Muslim authors. One of these movements, the 'Isawiyya, even recognized Muhammad as God's messenger to the Muslims. And in the end, some of what was viewed as heterodox or extremist by the majority of Jews found its way into the practices and ideas of certain Muslims.

In her essay in this volume, Tamar Frank identifies religious law as a point of commonality between Muslims and Jews, expressed through Shari'a in one case and Halakha in the other. The work of other scholars shows just how extensive and close the parallels are. Of course, some of Talmudic law actually reflects life under Muslim rule, just as some of the Shari'a reflects interaction with Jews or even the contributions of converts with a Jewish heritage.

In fact, the degree to which members of these two traditions have used divinely inspired law to regulate daily behavior, and the extent to which they have defined such discipline as a major form of piety, may not have a counterpart in any other religious community. So perhaps something that Jews and Muslims take for granted should not be taken for granted, and could even provide an important and constructive topic of interfaith conversation.

III. Al-Andalus

The Iberian Peninsula provided a somewhat different environment for intercommunal relations. Especially during the period when Muslims ruled most of the peninsula (tenth to thirteenth centuries), Jews were much influenced by Arab-Muslim culture and much involved in Muslim rule itself. Although officially in conflict, the Christian rulers in the north and the Muslim rulers in the south were socially and politically intertwined, and Jews often played a mediating role.

For example, in the mid-tenth century Toda, the queen mother of Navarre, was the grandmother of its future king, Sancho. However, she was also the great-aunt of the famous Umayyad Muslim ruler of Cordova, ‘Abd al-Rahman III. Toda's Christian grandson Sancho was too obese to ride a horse and thus to come to the throne, so Toda appealed to her Muslim great-nephew. The great-nephew, ‘Abd al-Rahman III, sent Hasdai ben Shaprut, his Jewish personal physician, to treat Sancho, in exchange for some of Toda's lands. Hasdai ben Shaprut brought Sancho back with him to Cordova, where he put him on a vegetarian diet and reduced his torso sufficiently so that he could sit a horse and, eventually, become king.

Hasdai ben Shaprut also became the first great patron of Hebrew letters, and in fact it is in the area of language and literature that Arab-Muslim culture had its greatest impact on Andalusian Jews. Arabic forms and metres influenced Hebrew secular poetry, and Arabic metres even came to be used in Hebrew religious poetry. The Jewish Andalusian style, developed by such famous poets as Ben Gabirol, Judah Halevi, and Avraham ben Ezra, spread to the Jewish communities of Babylonia, Egypt, North Africa, Palestine, Italy, Greece, Turkey, and Yemen. The Arabs' intense interest and skill in philology was one important source of inspiration for the revival of biblical Hebrew and the study of its grammar. Jewish writers frequently wrote in Judeo-Arabic (Arabic in Hebrew characters). Jewish philosophers like Maimonides were much influenced by reading philosophical texts written by Muslims in Arabic.

By the thirteenth century, al-Andalus, the territory under Muslim control, had begun to shrink very rapidly, and Muslims and Jews began to become minorities under Christian control. However, since at first the Christians treated them the way the Muslims had treated Jews and Christians, productive cooperation among the religious communities continued for some time. For example, Alfonso X of Castile (r. 1252-1284) styled himself "king of the three religions" and attempted to promote as much interaction as possible, especially through establishing a team of translators at Toledo. The Jews, knowing not only Hebrew and Arabic but also Castilian, now became natural intermediaries between Christians and Muslims. They also thus became central in the transmission to Europeans of Arabic folklore, literature, mathematics, science, and philosophy.

This period is in fact one of the few occasions in the history of the world in which Muslims and Jews lived as minorities under Christian domination in a relatively constructive way. However, that relationship did not survive the Christian domination of the peninsula. By the fifteenth century, Christian intolerance had begun to grow. The Jews were expelled in 1492; the Muslims, in 1609.

IV. The Ottoman Empire

The Ottoman Empire regularized and routinized the structure of faith communities even further, not only in the Middle East, but in North Africa and Europe as well. In so doing, it left a problematic legacy to the more than thirty modern nations that were born out of its dissolution. The transition from empire to nations was also exacerbated by British and French Mandate administration in the early twentieth century. In the Ottoman Empire, religious communities were joined together and kept in balance only by the administrative control of the Sultan, but otherwise left largely to regulate their own communal life. In the British and French Mandates, the religious communities were often set against each other, and their social and economic power reallocated. The borders drawn for the new nation-states often created further intercommunal tensions, and the demand for all citizens to be equal before the same law was difficult to meet. Even in today's Israel, citizenship is distinguished from nationality, which is based on religious affiliation, and quasi-autonomous legal systems are recognized for a number of religious communities. In fact, the tensions between Israelis and Arabs, or between Muslims and Jews, have been caused more by these relatively recent factors than by any age-old inevitable rivalries.

V. Conclusion

From this brief historical survey we can make two observations: 1) The United States is not the first place in which Jews and Muslims have lived as minorities in a culture dominated by another religion, but it *is* the first time they have lived together as minorities in a society that celebrates pluralism, and insists on the equality of all faith communities under a single legal system and a single national identity. 2) Just as Jewish-Muslim relations have adapted to other changes in the past, they should be able to adapt to this one. The history of Jewish-Muslim interaction provides us with enough resources to make the kind of creative adaptations so often required of Jews and Muslims in the past.

We can learn from history; we are not its prisoner. The situation in which we find ourselves is not characteristic of any period in the history of our interactions with each other, and we are free to make creative adaptations of our traditions to the present situation. However, since Jews have rarely lived as a majority or as the dominant culture anywhere, this situation is less unprecedented for them. Still, their challenge will be to learn to live with Muslims on new terms. The Islamic tradition, on the other hand, has developed from very different historical experiences, for Muslims have generally lived in cultures in which they have predominated, and much of the Islamic tradition is based on that kind of social assumption. So Muslims will be challenged to find not only new ways to live as neighbors with Jews, but authentic ways to live as a minority in a culture dominated by another tradition altogether.

ENDNOTES

[1]William M. Brinner, and Stephen D. Ricks (eds.), *Studies in Islamic and Judaic Traditions* (Brown Judaic Studies 110; Atlanta, 1986).

[2]Marilyn Robinson Waldman, *Toward a Theory of Historical Narrative* (Columbus, OH, 1980), 179.

SUGGESTIONS FOR FURTHER READING

Goitein, S.D. *Jews and Arabs: Their Contacts Through the Ages*. New York, 1964.

Jackson, Gabriel. *The Making of Medieval Spain*. New York, 1972.

Newby, Gordon Darnell. *A History of the Jews of Arabia*. Columbia, SC, 1989.

MARILYN ROBINSON WALDMAN is Professor of History and Comparative Studies at The Ohio State University. She received her Ph.D. in History from The University of Chicago (1974).

SCRIPTURE AND COMMUNITY

Tamar Frank

Dialogue is always a tricky affair. From trivial exchanges about everyday matters to the proverbially difficult areas of religion and politics, even the most sensitive and self-aware must constantly remember to listen, to understand the other viewpoint, to re-evaluate ideas held as axiomatic. The staged debates of the medieval period, when scholars of different faiths were invited to a court to present arguments for the superiority of different points of view, are hardly a model for interfaith discourse today. Yet how many of us allow assumptions about the way "we" do things or what "they" believe to go unchallenged? Perhaps greater understanding is the most that we can expect from interfaith dialogue; to me it seems like a great deal. Certainly, an understanding of similarities and differences among religious traditions, an increased knowledge of shared or diverse traditions, can only enhance the possibility of future dialogue.

It is perhaps a commonplace that the Jewish and Islamic traditions have many points of similarity. Let us consider a process of evolution and development that appears similar in these two communities. This parallel process will also show that both communities are similar in the things they hold important and in the ways they respond to new problems and ideas. Please read the word "similar" carefully: I am not implying the influence of one tradition upon the other, nor do I mean "identical." I mean, rather, that the similarities discussed here between the two traditions are so striking as to enhance future possibilities for dialogue and reflection.

We know that Judaism and Islam are "religions of the Book": each of these sister faiths has its origin in a revelation that was codified in scripture. We know, too, that each of these faiths has a normative interpretation of that scripture, or perhaps, an authoritative mechanism by which scripture can be interpreted. Let us look, then, at three reference points to see what they indicate about the growth of these traditions. They are prophecy, scripture, and authoritative interpretation.

I. Prophecy

The revelations which gave the impetus to Islam came over a short period of time, some twenty years, to a single person, the Prophet Muhammad. The various texts which compose the Hebrew Bible cover a time span of perhaps a thousand years and the experiences of many individuals. Despite this difference, however, there are some remarkable similarities in prophetic message and experience.

One prominent theme in both cases, for example, is the divine call for social justice. Look for example at Amos' injunction to LET JUSTICE WELL UP LIKE WATER (5:24) and at his indictment of those who have become wealthy at the expense of the poor and downtrodden. Jeremiah, too, speaks of WICKED MEN whose HOUSES ARE FULL OF GUILE; they PASS BEYOND THE BOUNDS OF WICKEDNESS for THEY WILL NOT JUDGE THE CASE OF THE ORPHAN NOR GIVE A HEARING TO THE PLEA OF THE NEEDY (5:26ff).

Muhammad, too, from early in his prophetic mission, brings a message of divine retribution against those who mistreat the poor and defenseless. The Qur'an's Sura (Chapter) 108, the Sura "Charity," warns WOE . . . TO THOSE WHO MAKE DISPLAY AND REFUSE CHARITY, that is, those WHO REPULSE THE ORPHAN AND URGE NOT THE FEEDING OF THE NEEDY. The people singled out for protection in the qur'anic message, as in the Bible, are those with no "protection network" or power of their own in traditional Middle Eastern societies: women, orphans, the poor, sometimes strangers. In fact, the social message of the Qur'an was concretized by the extension of the idea of kinship group to the *umma*, the community of faith. This new entity, a revolutionary social change for sixth-century Arabia, was intended to become a "family" of believers whose members would be responsible for one another.

In addition to the social message brought by both Old Testament prophets and Muhammad, we discover similarities in other aspects of their messages. An emphasis on the generosity of God, on His willingness to accept those who hear Him, and the moving use of natural imagery (God's generosity to humankind in its most visible form) are found in both revelations.

Finally, the persona of prophet has many shared aspects. The prophet himself is reluctant to receive his call: Isaiah, for example, protests that his LIPS [ARE] UNCLEAN (6:5); Jeremiah tries to refuse his call with the words, I AM STILL A BOY (1:6). Muhammad, too, reacts in this way to his first revelation--with a refusal, or an inability to repeat the word "Recite!" which the angel Gabriel finally shakes out of him. His biography, or *sira*, preserves a story of his fear that his revelation might not be a true one. (See for example, Suras 96, 74, and traditions concerning the first revelations.)

The old proverb about a "prophet without honor in his own country" applies, again, both to our Hebrew prophets and to Muhammad. Amos was accused by Amaziah, the priest, of conspiring against the king, and told not to prophesy in THE KING'S SANCTUARY (7:12); Jeremiah, of course, was imprisoned, and the revealed messages which he dictated to his scribe were destroyed at the king's command. Muhammad's revelations, at least initially, were greeted with hostility and derision by many of his kinsmen and other citizens of Mecca. Even after he had gathered a group of followers and they had established themselves in Medina, he had to lead military campaigns to win both territory and the right to make a pilgrimage to the Meccan sanctuary.

Another point of similarity is the notion of revealed law, and of the prophet as lawgiver. This is not the place for an examination either of biblical or of qur'anic law, but we can make the point that, in each case, what the community of the faithful receives on the prophet's authority is a core of revealed legal material that will be elaborated by the community through commentary, analogy, and other authorized means. We will look at some of these methods a bit later.

We should also acknowledge here the idea of the prophet himself as a leader of his community and even as a judge during his own lifetime. Moses as lawgiver and leader, Joshua as military commander, and the Israelite judges are biblical examples; Muhammad, of course, ruled his community of Muslims and led them in battle during his lifetime.

In both message and circumstances, then, we can see some similarities in the prophetic impulse behind our two "daughters of Abraham." Let us turn next to the scripture that grew from these prophetic impulses.

II. Scripture

The canonization of the Hebrew scriptures was a lengthy process, taking works from many different periods and of many different types and combining them into a book that could be thought of as a unified whole. The Qur'an was redacted in less than a generation and consists of materials revealed in a single prophetic voice. Nevertheless, each text functions for its community in a similar way: it is the ultimate validation of the community's experience. Put in a simpler way, without a Book, there is no Community, no sense of a group bound together by a God-given message. Both traditions are very conscious of the centrality of the written message. In fact, the Qur'an is full of references to scriptural revelation, to the Book itself, to the Preserved Tablet, some of which probably date from a time when Muhammad's revelations were first orally preserved.

Now it is easy to see that a community with a living prophetic voice is vital and growing. So, too, a community in the process of editing, arranging, sorting, and compiling the records of such voices. But how have these two communities remained dynamic throughout the long period following the closing of scripture? What mechanism have they for "hearing" the divine, following the right path, and doing the proper thing in the absence of living prophetic guidance?

III. Authoritative Interpretation

The answer to these questions, of course, is "interpretation," but this is an answer we must qualify. Surely, any interpretation will not do; there must be a way to determine a course of action that can be sanctioned within the community. And here both of our communities, the Jewish and Muslim, have a remarkably similar way of dealing with new questions, new situations, and new movements. Let us consider the concepts of "Torah" and "Sunna" and the way in which they function in their respective communities.

The word Torah, of course, is used to designate the Pentateuch, the Five Books of Moses. Let us look at the word itself, and how it came to mean these things and much more. Originally, the word *torah* was a legal term, and meant a specific decision in a specific legal case. By extension, it came to mean the general principle by which that decision was made, that is, a law. By further extension, it came to mean the general principle that such principles--or laws--exist, that is, the notion of Law itself. Hence, it came to mean a teaching or a tradition. So it was applied to the Pentateuch, that part of the Bible that contains the laws God gave to Moses.

It came to mean more still. When God tells Isaiah to BIND UP THE MESSAGE AND SEAL THE INSTRUCTION [that is, *torah*] WITH MY DISCIPLES, the reference is to the whole of God's plan for the world, to the totality of revelation and experience. Prophecy, then, is Torah--so is the whole of the biblical canon. Torah is the total of authoritative teachings, teachings whose authority and formulation precede their use by the tradition. But as we can easily see, authoritative teachings must include both the law and its interpretation. Even the clearest-seeming of laws can admit problems; what about laws that do not seem clear at all?

A biblical example is the problematic divorce law in Deuteronomy 24:1-4, which would pose serious practical problems without some kind of interpretation. Readers familiar with qur'anic law might think of the inheritance laws, and of the generations of children who have had to work out trigonometry and sums by trying to divide a man's field among his heirs. Yes, the communities must try to live by the laws God gave them, but they must have some kind of guidelines, an interpretation that is somehow sanctioned, in order to apply these laws to their own situations.

The idea of an authorized interpretation gave rise, among Jews, to the idea of the Oral Torah, that is, the traditional, community-authorized interpretation. Of course, this approach was not without problems. Which, of the many oral *torah*s, was the one to follow? The position of the teacher of the Law began to take on great importance: people would follow a particular interpretation because of a scholar's reputation for rectitude and knowledge, so that his practice might be followed even when his reasons for it were not known or had been lost with time.

A phenomenon arose that will seem very familiar to those who know about the *hadith* and the idea of *isnad*, that is, a chain of transmission. Interpretations were cited in the name of a particular scholar, and his whole scholarly lineage would be set out in authentication. The sage became the new figure of authority; no longer was it the hereditary priesthood that established the community norms, but the sages. The important connections were one's teachers, rather than one's family.

What we see is the gradual development of a kind of circle: Torah needs the Tradition for its continued life and authority; Torah (the fixed, the past) remains part of Tradition (the living, the present); finally, the living tradition becomes part of Torah. That is, the Written Torah, the Scriptures themselves, are not to be thought of in the absence of Oral Torah, the commentaries and interpretations. And finally, the Oral Torah became a written collection itself, a text to be studied in its own right. So the legal directives, decisions, legends, homilies, commentaries of various kinds that had been passed on in the academies came to be collected as the Talmud, the subject of study by subsequent generations. An apt expression of this dynamic is the Sephardic saying that all Jewish literature is the interrelation between text, *hibbur*, and commentary, *perush*: the history of Jewish literature is the history of *perushim* becoming *hibburim*.

Of course, the process did not stop there. The tradition continued to grow and change, to meet challenges, and finally, to incorporate ideas, trends, or movements that originated in opposition to it, but of this, more later.

I would like to turn now to the development of the concept of *sunna*, a process that is strikingly similar to the one we have just seen. After the death of Muhammad, the need was felt to collect the revelations from wherever they could be found: "whether written on palm leaves or flat stones or in the hearts of men," as the tradition tells us.

As in the case of the Hebrew Bible, where the establishment of the best possible text was the first step in the scholarly tradition (1st c. before the Common Era [BCE]-2nd c. of the Common Era [CE]), the Islamic scholarly tradition began by assembling a Qur'an text that would be normative. The establishment of a definitive text, one that would be recognized and used by the entire community, was in itself a kind of interpretation, the first step in constituting and asserting an authoritative voice for the community.

It was in the formulation and development of the ideas of *hadith* and *sunna* that the community really found a voice. A *hadith* is a verbal communication, a bit of news or a news report; it has come to mean "a tradition," specifically, "a prophetic tradition," a report about something that the Prophet Muhammad did or said. Of course, a saying or an action of Muhammad would provide an example of appropriate behavior, whether the case might be the giving of charity, the repetition of a particular prayer, or even the use of a comb at certain times. These doings and sayings were recorded in two-part formulas, the *isnad*, or chain of transmission documenting the saying (and remember the Talmudic sages above), and the *matn*, the content of the tradition.

However, even these *hadith*s did not cover all cases or provide interpretations for all difficulties, and we come now to the concept *sunna*. Here, as in the case of the word and concept *torah*, the Muslim community was making use of an older term and idea. *Sunna* means a well trodden path, that is, the way of older generations, the customary way of doing things. For the new Muslim community, it referred first to the Prophet's own *sunna*, to his way of doing things, then to the *sunna* of his Companions and the Successors; finally, it came to mean the *sunna*, the customary way, of the generations that followed, that is, the traditional way or the norm of the community. As in the case of the Talmud, the collections of traditions and legal materials came to be the objects of study in their own right; the commentaries themselves were commented upon and studied in schools, epitomes were gradually made, and these became the primary texts for study, and so on.

As the study of Islamic law, or *shari'a*, became formalized, the idea of the four roots of law took hold, especially as defined by al-Shafi'i (d. 820 CE). Using these "roots" or principles in sequence, or so the theory is, any legal problem can be solved. First, of course, comes the Qur'an, then the Sunna. If recourse to these sources will not solve a particular problem, a scholar may use *ijtihad*, personal effort at interpretation in the form of *qiyas* (a very strict kind of analogical reasoning).

Let us now examine the fourth, or last, root: *ijma'*, the consensus of the community. This notion concretizes a dynamic discussed above in connection with Judaism: the symbiosis between the community and its authorized interpreters. This relationship is not usually based on formal titles, certainly not on titles alone, but rather on the respect accorded to particular scholars, or to the scholarly establishment, and on the community's willingness to acccept interpretations. Both of the communities we are considering--the Muslim and Jewish communities particularly during the medieval period--were more interested in accommodation than in exclusivity. That is, they wanted to keep believers within the fold, and, in general, the fold could be made to hold many different shades of opinion and practice. But of course, there were always checks on radical, self-serving, or partisan interpretations. In the long run, the mechanism of *ijma'*, of consensus, brought the extremes in toward the middle.

The idea of a new movement that gradually becomes the mainstream or establishment is a familiar one, and in the case of the Jewish and Islamic traditions, we see this process again. As the normative traditions grew more and more scholastic and legalistic, as the study of religion and religious texts became more and more a process of learning what commentators had written about previous commentaries on commentaries, both traditions saw the growth of movements concerned with spiritual renewal.

At first, there were only individuals, then a few teachers with their disciples, who sought to recapture the immediacy of the prophetic experience, the initial impulse behind the words of the scriptures. While realizing, in the case of each of these two traditions, that prophecy was closed, that God would not choose a new human voice, these people sought an experiential, rather than a scholastic, knowledge of the divine: these people, of course, were the mystics.

However, in the Talmudic period--in fact, the Talmud itself contains texts that reflect mystical ideas and experiences--and into the medieval period, Jewish mysticism existed in a guarded and secretive way. Both because of the danger of mystical experimentation to the uninitiated, and because of the potential heterodoxy of the mystics' ideas, mysticism was frowned on and discouraged by the community authorities. Judaism saw the growth of a number of mystical movements: the *merkabah* mysticism of the early texts, the Zoharic *kabbalah* of the Spanish period, the Lurianic *kabbalah* of the sixteenth century, and the development of Hasidism in the seventeenth century.

The early movements began as esoteric ones, strictly for the initiates whose level of understanding was adequate to instruction in the mysteries of coded texts and mystical encounters; Hasidism, on the other hand, was more a movement of social revolution, since it invited the participation of worshippers who were not necessarily strong in "book-learning" but ready to praise God in any way they could, in song, dance, and story. Both types of movement reflect a dissatisfaction with what was perceived as a static and legalistic tradition, far removed from the divine voice that spoke through the words of Torah. Both types of movement, too, were met with intense hostility; the leaders were chastised for leading the faithful into error, and the followers were exhorted to mend their ways and return to the community.

However, the consensus mechanism of the community worked to normalize the extreme by inclusion. A few specific examples: some of the most famous (and beautiful) hymns and liturgical poems--now part of every mainstream Sabbath liturgy--are the product of these different mystical groups. The frequently-used image of the Sabbath as a beautiful bride, again, is a legacy from the Lurianic kabbalists of sixteenth-century Palestine. And the Hasidim, some of whose songs are used by most congregations in North America, are hardly revolutionaries any more, but are rather seen as the arch-conservatives of Judaism.

Among Muslims, too, a mystical movement--or sequence of mystical movements--arose as early as the eighth century, associated with the label "Sufi." Led by pious figures who were already mourning the "golden age" of pure faith barely one hundred years before, a movement toward asceticism gradually took on mystical coloring. The ascetics were at least tolerated, and often respected, great figures like Hasan al-Basri (d. 728 CE) or Harith al-Muhasibi (d. 837 CE); but with the coming of a more ecstatic mysticism, the community, or what could be called the orthodox establishment, began to get uneasy. Abu Yazid al-Bistami's ecstatic utterances, the *dhikr* rituals of ecstasy-inducing dancing and chanting, and the antinomian (anti-legalistic) tendencies of some of the other mystics created a climate of hostility and distrust on the part of the establishment that led, finally, to the execution of the most famous, and perhaps the most scandalous of the early mystics, al-Hallaj (d. 922 CE).

Surely, one might think, this kind of event would decide, once and for all, the community's consensus against mysticism. But once again, we see the wonderful dynamic of a religious community. The struggle among Muslims between intellectualized faith and mysticism was personified by the figure of al-Ghazali (d. 1111 CE), whose life both exemplified and guided the community's evolution. Having studied *falsafa* (which included Greek and Greek-influenced philosophy and the natural sciences) and the Islamic religious sciences, he felt that his life--and perhaps the life of the community--was at a standstill. The spiritual refreshment and renewal he found through a period spent in mystical retreat was also expressed in his great compendium, *Ihya' 'ulum al-din*, *The Revival of Religious Sciences*. In this guide, he showed how a reflective or meditative dimension can be introduced into all religious duties and obligations, and even into the most mundane aspects of life. His personal experience and recognition of the mystical way--together with an emphasis on "sober" mysticism and on meditative discipline--gave the definitive expression of legitimacy to a tendency or movement that was gaining ground within the community.

IV. Conclusion

This all too hasty look at the development of the Islamic and Jewish traditions should have served at least one function, that of showing that a religious community cannot be a static entity. Living traditions, like living  things, are characterized by organic growth, by changes that develop within the tradition. Even in responding to external challenges, these traditions use their own means, their own scriptures, their own *sunna* or *torah*, their own customary way of doing things. We have seen that through the circle of scripture and traditional interpretation, these communities have a great potential for evolution, and it will be interesting to see, too, how these communities change in the future.

In North America, where religious communities are close neighbors and interact more, perhaps, than in many other parts of the world, we have seen in the past tendencies toward liberalization and toleration, as well as an emphasis on civic virtues and on participation in the greater community. Let us hope that, whatever direction our communites take in the future, they will remain open to dialogues and to cooperation for the public benefit.

SUGGESTIONS FOR FURTHER READING

Arberry, A.J. *Sufism*. London, 1950.

Blenkinsopp, J. *Prophecy and Canon: A Contribution to the Study of Jewish Origins*. Notre Dame, 1977.

Heschel, A.J. *The Prophets*. New York, 1962.

Rahman, F. *Islam*, second edition. Chicago, 1979.

____. *Major Themes of the Qur'an*. Minneapolis, 1980.

Schimmel, A. *Mystical Dimensions of Islam*. Chapel Hill, 1975.

Scholem, G. "Religious Authority and Mysticism." In *On the Kabbalah and its Symbolism* (tr. R. Manheim). New York, 1965.

Urbach, E. "The Talmudic Sage--Character and Authority." In H. H. Ben-Sasson and S. Ettinger (eds.), *Jewish Society Through the Ages*. New York, 1971.

Watt, W.M. *The Faith and Practice of al-Ghazali*. London, 1953.

TAMAR FRANK is Program Consultant to the Maurice Amado Foundation Sephardic Education Project in Cincinnati, Ohio. She received her Ph.D. in Medieval Studies from Yale University (1975).

HISTORICAL PERSPECTIVES ON CHRISTIAN-MUSLIM RELATIONS

Marilyn Robinson Waldman

We all know that comparative religion can be a tricky business, and the one story I know about Muslim-Christian interaction makes that point very well. It is a story about a famous Muslim folk hero who goes by many names but is here called Mulla Nasrudin:

> Nasrudin put on a Sufi robe and decided to make a pious journey. On his way he met a [Christian] priest and a[n Indian] yogi, and they decided to team up together. When they got to a village the others asked him to seek donations while they carried out their devotions. Nasrudin collected some money and bought halwa with it.
>
> He suggested that they divide the food, but the others, who were not yet hungry enough, said that it should be postponed until night. They continued on their way; and when night fell Nasrudin asked for the first portion "because I was the means of getting the food." The others disagreed: the priest on the grounds that he represented a properly organized hierarchical body, and should therefore have preference; the yogi because, he said, he ate only once in three days and should therefore have more.
>
> Finally they decided to sleep. In the morning, the one who related the best dream should have first choice of the halwa.

> In the morning the priest said: "In my dreams I saw the founder of my religion, who made a sign of benediction, singling me out as especially blessed."
>
> The others were impressed, but the Yogi said: "I dreamt that I visited Nirvana, and was utterly absorbed into nothing."
>
> They turned to the Mulla. "I dreamt that I saw the Sufi teacher Khidr, who appears only to the most sanctified [and to whom Sufis owe complete obedience]."
>
> "He said, 'Nasrudin, eat the halwa--now!' And, of course, I had to obey."[1]

This is not only a very good Mulla story, but it also suggests that there are many surprises in store for those who study the interaction of religious communities. The story also implicitly suggests some of the new perspectives that most Americans will need to adopt in order to make sense of the history of Muslim-Christian interaction. The way the world is right now, and especially the way American society is organized and the assumptions that it makes about religious affiliation, do not automatically provide adequate vantage points for thinking about the history of Muslim-Christian interaction around the world during the last 1400 years. There are at least four unfamiliar facts that we will need to bear in mind.

I. The Significance of Eastern Christianity

The history of Muslim-Christian interaction involves eastern or othodox forms of Christianity as much as western forms of Christianity, a fact that is usually ignored. Most people who have grown up in the United States would probably assume that the priest in the Mulla story is a Catholic priest, but he is much more likely to have belonged to some form of eastern Christianity. Yet most Americans do not ever learn enough about the history of Christianity as a global phenomenon to know what it was like in the areas where Islam arose (i.e., northwestern Arabia) and to which it quickly spread (i.e., westward to Egypt, North Africa, and Spain; northward into the "Middle East"; and eastward into Iran and Central Asia).

Furthermore, a knowledge of Christianity's current demography, in the world or in the United States, is not very helpful for putting ourselves back into northwestern Arabia and its environs at the beginning of the seventh century and in the centuries that followed. At the present time, large numbers of Christians live in the western hemisphere, and Christian identification is increasing rapidly in the rest of the world as well. Because of that fact, Harvey Cox has begun to predict that Christianity will become more of a "third-world" religion in the next millennium, and that one of the next few popes will be Latin American or African.

In the United States about 56% of all Christians are Protestant and about 33% are Roman Catholic. So Americans tend to forget, or never notice, that world-wide 56% of Christians are Roman Catholic and only 20% Protestant. I once asked a middle school class in north Columbus how many of the world's Christians are Roman Catholic, and they said "Oh, about 10%."

The current global expansion of Christianity, the numerical superiority of Roman Catholics worldwide, and the numerical superiority of Protestants in the United States, constitute a reality very different from that in which Islam arose. In the year 600, on the eve of the Prophet Muhammad's first encounter with God, there were relatively few Christians living west of Rome, because the Christian faith had not yet spread significantly westward from its eastern Mediterranean homelands. There were no Roman Catholics or Protestants per se, because the Protestant Reformation was 900 years away. The majority of Christians belonged, at least officially, to one Church, because the Great Schism had not yet been finalized; and many of its members were loyal to the Patriarch at Constantinople, not to the Bishop of Rome, even when he began to call himself the Pope. Most Christians lived in the Later Roman Empire, whose seventh-century capital was Constantinople, and many Christians practiced forms of Christianity unfamiliar to most Americans--Coptic, Nestorian, Monophysite, and so forth.

In Arabia, and in many other areas to which Islam spread, we are not entirely sure what Christianity was actually like, despite the efforts of many scholars. However, recent research on Syriac Christianity to the north of Arabia in the seventh century indicates that Christianity in that part of the world may have been much more similar to what is described in the Qur'an than has usually been thought. Many western scholars have argued that the Qur'an "got Christianity wrong," because it describes Christianity in a way different from our understanding; but those few scholars who work on the Christianity of Syriac-speakers to the north (Syriac being a Semitic language closely related to Arabic) have discovered that many things that characterize common Syriac Christian practice are similar to practices and ideas attributed to Christians in the Qur'an.

In Arabia, Christianity was presumably a minority religion when Islam arose; but in many of the areas to which Islam spread outside Arabia, Christianity was the majority religion. And many Christians in that part of the world used Syriac or Arabic in their worship, not Greek or Latin. So when we say Christian-Muslim interaction, we have to know what we mean by "Christian," and that is not always easy to do.

II. The Longevity of Muslim-Christian Interaction

Muslims and Christians have lived together and interacted with each other for a very long time, in fact since the emergence of Islam in northwest Arabia early in the seventh century of the Common Era. In many other parts of the world and at many other times, they have not been so foreign to each other as they tend to be in the United States. It is not the case that there was no polemic, that there was complete understanding; but it is the case that Muslims and Christians of this part of the world were probably better able to converse with each other than we are in the United States. For example, it would have been much easier for Muslim and Christian scholars in Damascus in the eighth century to have a theological discussion than it would be for us, because Muslims and Christians in the parts of the world in which interaction has primarily taken place often spoke "a common language," in either the figurative or literal sense of the term. There were Arab Christians in the environs of Muhammad's community, some of whom became Muslim. Figures who appear in the Christian Bible also appear in the Qur'an. Since the earliest Muslims viewed Islam as the natural and original religion, they believed that all messengers of God had brought essentially the same message, which culminated in Muhammad.

During the first 200 years of Muslim expansion and rule in the Middle East, Muslims only very gradually became a majority of the population in the areas they controlled, largely through the peaceful absorption of large numbers of Christians and a much smaller number of Jews. In fact, the transformation of this area from predominantly Christian to predominantly Muslim is one of the most understudied major cultural transformations in human history. In the course of it, many of these new Muslims or children of new Muslims became important figures in the development of Islamic thought and culture. Conversely, Islamic thought influenced the ongoing development of Christian thought as well. For example, it is thought that the attempt by an eighth-century Byzantine emperor to ban the use of icons was influenced by familiarity with Muslim prohibitions on the use of images in worship. Furthermore, the Muslim view of Jesus as messenger of God rather than son of God had precedents in certain early Christian views that had not become part of mainstream Christianity, and caused Arab Christians to redefine their notions of prophecy. We have Syriac Christian accounts of the rise of Islam that are earlier than the earliest surviving accounts written by Muslims in Arabic. Christian architects helped to build some of the first mosques (Muslim places of prayer). Raymond Llull, the famous fourteenth-century Christian-Majorcan scholar and writer, knew Arabic better than he knew Latin, and was influenced by Muslim Sufis (as well as the Jewish Maimonides). The earliest European universities may well have been influenced by Muslim schools in locales like Sicily. To this day, as in the past, many Arab Christians who use an Arabic translation of the Christian Bible and call God "Allah," are well aware of the Muslim understanding of that term even though they understand it differently.

A particularly important site of Muslim-Christian interaction was the Ottoman empire, which expanded into southeastern Europe in the fifteenth and sixteenth centuries. Most of the Ottoman ruling class, at least in these early centuries, was composed not of Turks or of Muslims, but of Christian youths who were "drafted," converted to Islam, and trained in the Ottoman language and in Ottoman administrative and military skills. It is this expansion, by the way, that produced today's Muslim communities of countries like Yugoslavia or Bulgaria or Albania. In the Ottoman Empire, Christian communities were quite various, and the different Christian communities came to be associated with different ethnicities or nationalities.

Furthermore, most Muslim-Christian relationships in the past have to be put under the heading of some kind of co-existence, rather than conflict. Where conflict has occurred, it has originated as much on the Christian side as on the Muslim side. Here again, the instances of Muslim-Christian conflict that Americans know best, the Crusades of the eleventh and twelfth centuries, and the era of European colonialism in the nineteenth and twentieth centuries, do not provide adequate models for understanding the whole sweep of Christian-Muslim interaction. In those cases, Europeans went to a predominantly Muslim part of the world and tried, unsuccessfully, to conquer it. Similarly, the major instances of Muslim expansion into Christian lands--the Middle East and North Africa in the seventh century, Spain in the eighth century, and the Later Roman, or Byzantine, Empire in the fifteenth century--are not adequate models either.

For despite obvious instances of conflict involving force, most Muslims and Christians have coexisted, sometimes uneasily, sometimes with very positive cultural results, as in Spain (both during the period of extensive Muslim control and in areas that first came under Christian domination). Even the Crusades, which we identify with violence and forced contact, probably promoted a great deal of interaction as well: we are just beginning to know about the influence of the Muslim east on medieval Europe's literature, art, education, and music; and it came about even in an instance where violence was the intended result of the contact.

One of the most unusual examples of Muslim-Christian encounter occurred in the Philippines in the sixteenth century. It illustrates the extent of the peaceful expansion of Islam through trade and commerce and preaching, but also the negative reaction of European Christians to it. After the Spanish made their conquests in the New World, some of them sailed across from Mexico to what became the Philippines. When the Spaniards reached what is now Manila, they were shocked to find Muslims from the south, who had come up from Java and Borneo, converting large numbers of locals to Islam. When the Spaniards encountered these Muslims, who were a mixture of Middle Eastern and Indian Ocean peoples, they referred to them as the Moros (their label to the present day); that is, they referred to them with the same name they had used in Spain--Moros, the Moors. One can imagine their shock, just having conquered the last Muslim stronghold of Granada in 1492, and thinking they had gotten Muslims under control, coming halfway around the world and finding them there.

It is important to remember that even before northern European Christians began their attempt to reconquer the Holy Land from Muslims, Spanish Christians had begun to reconquer the Iberian Peninsula from Muslims. Ironically, the conquest Americans tend to know more about, and make more of--the assault on the Holy Land--"failed," whereas the one Americans are very little interested in, the conquest of Spain, "succeeded."

The Spanish experience in the Philippines also suggests a different view of 1492, and a different perspective on the Quincentenary which celebrates it. It reminds us that Muslim peoples were still economically powerful at the time of the New World explorations. After all, Christopher Columbus was really seeking a route to the east when he stumbled on the Americas, a route that would allow Europeans to bypass Muslim and other middlemen in the Indian Ocean trade. The year 1492 was significant not only for Columbus' landing in the New World, but also for the fall of Granada and the subsequent expansion of Spaniards into the Indian Ocean itself. So the second point is, one cannot disentangle the history of Muslim and Christian communities in the world no matter how hard one tries.

III. Christians as Subject Communities

Unlike the United States, where Muslims are a small but increasingly visible minority living in a predominantly Christian environment, in most places where Muslims and Christians have lived together in the past, Muslims have predominated politically, and usually numerically, and Christians have been minority communities. Much less often have Muslims been minority communities in predominantly Christian lands. Usually where Muslims were minorities in Christian lands, they were the rulers anyway despite the numerical inferiority.

Following the pre-Islamic practice of the empires that they began to conquer in the mid-seventh century, Muslims tended to organize the population for social and political purposes along the lines of religious affiliation, classifying non-Muslim communities as *dhimmis* (protected minorities). This system reached its height under the Ottomans, who extended their rule from Anatolia to Europe in the fifteenth and sixteenth centuries (conquering Constantinople in 1453) and to Arabic-speaking North Africa and Middle East in the sixteenth and seventeenth centuries. So the third point is, the American reality of Muslims living as minorities in Christian lands reverses the historical picture, in which Muslims have generally lived either as a majority ruling over a Christian minority, or even as a minority ruling over a Christian majority. The American situation is a novel one, both full of pitfalls but also full of opportunities.

IV. Religion as Nationality

As a result of organizing people into religious communities, in the major areas of Christian-Muslim interaction, religious labels have also functioned differently than in the United States, more the way they function for Catholics and Protestants in Northern Ireland, as symbols of much broader cultural, social, and political identities. This same social organization that helped the various communities under Muslim rule coexist, has unfortunately, as we have seen in recent years, also contributed to new kinds of conflict, most notably in places like Lebanon, which at the time of its creation by the French had one of the most complicated sets of religious communities in the region. Much Middle Eastern "religious" conflict in recent years can in fact be traced to the difficult transition from loosely-held clusters of virtually self-governing religious communities to nation-states, with their expectations of equality before a single secular national law and the relegation of religious identity exclusively to the private sphere.

Another story well illustrates this pattern of using religion as a shorthand for cultural differences, and even as an indicator of ethnicity and nationality. It was told to me by Alford Carleton, who worked with the World Council of Churches in the British Mandate of Palestine during most of the interwar years. One day Mr. Carleton (a tall, thin, fair, blond patrician-looking person) found himself crossing the Bosphorus in a ferry boat with a Turkish Muslim. The Turkish Muslim could not speak English and my friend, an American Presbyterian, could not speak Turkish. But they both spoke French, and in the conversation that ensued they became so friendly so fast that the Turkish Muslim said to the American Presbyterian, "nous musulmanes," "we Muslims." My friend feared the possible consequences of participating in this deception, so he said, "Excuse me, sir, I'm sorry to have to tell you I'm not a Muslim." And the Muslim said "Well, then, what are you?" And my friend said, with some trepidation, "Well, I'm a Christian." And the Muslim looked at him in disbelief and said, "That's funny; you don't look a bit Armenian!" Being an heir to the Ottoman Empire, the Turk could imagine a pale, European-looking Muslim, but he couldn't imagine a generic Christian apart from a specific ethnic-religious community. Religion and nationality, religion and ethnicity, have a connection in the Middle East, and elsewhere, that they do not have in the United States, and not understanding that connection is an obstacle to understanding the Middle East. However, in this case, Middle Eastern tradition is not a very good resource for building intercommunal relations in America; in fact, one of the challenges for Americans--Muslims and Christians alike--is to understand religious communities in a different way from the way in which they have functioned historically in the areas in which Muslims and Christians have most come in contact with each other.

It is clear even from this brief and superficial sketch of a very complicated topic, that Muslim-Christian interaction has come in a variety of forms. The image of the Crusades as the primary way that Christians and Muslims have related simply is not adequate to the task. Historical study shows that all things are possible, from tragic conflict to tolerance to mutually creative interaction. I know that it is traditional for Americans to repeat the line, "Those who do not know history are condemned to repeat it." But that is not the way I think about history. My line is, "Those who do not know history are closed off from the opportunities that it presents." I think the knowledge of history shows us that all things are possible for us. However, a note of caution: as I mentioned earlier, we are a moment in this long history; we are not separate from it. What we do in and with this volume will become part of the history of Muslim-Christian interaction. We may be trying to stand at a distance to look at it, but we are also part of it, and what we do will affect its course. This is the first time in human history that Muslims have been called upon to live as a permanent minority in a predominantly Christian land with a pluralistic value system. That is the challenge on the Muslim side. The challenge for the non-Muslim American is to question the long-held assumption that religious pluralism is captured in the phrase "Protestant, Catholic, Jew." The presence not only of Muslim-Americans, but also of Buddhist-Americans and Hindu-Americans, Bahai-Americans, Jain-Americans, and so forth, demands that non-Muslim-American citizens as well as Muslim-American citizens rethink the history of Muslim-Christian interaction, and, I hope, take the opportunity to contribute to it in perhaps the most creative way yet.

ENDNOTES

[1] Idries Shah (ed.), *The Pleasantries of the Incomparable Mulla Nasrudin* (New York, 1971), 75.

SUGGESTIONS FOR FURTHER READING

Hick, John and Edmund S. Meltzer (eds.). *Three Faiths--One God: A Jewish, Christian, Muslim Encounter*. Albany, 1989.

Speight, R. Marston. *Christian-Muslim Relations, An Introduction for Christians in the* U.S.A. 3rd edition; Office on Christian-Muslim Relations of the National Council of Churches, 1983.

Usamah ibn Munqidh (tr. Philip K. Hitti). *Memoirs of an Arab-Syrian Gentleman of the Crusades or An Arab Knight in the Crusades*. New York, 1929; Beirut, 1964.

MARILYN ROBINSON WALDMAN is Professor of History and Comparative Studies at The Ohio State University. She received her Ph.D. in History from the University of Chicago (1974).

PART III

SOCIETY: THE RELIGIOUS COMMUNITIES IN AMERICA

CHRISTIANS AS A MAJORITY IN THE UNITED STATES

Thomas Templeton Taylor

I will begin by examining some ambiguities in the idea of a Christian majority, and then will try to report on one way of organizing the bewildering array of Christian groups in America into a coherent pattern, using an important recent book by sociologists Wade Clark Roof and William McKinney. Toward the end, I will make some observations on contemporary Christianity, drawing on the work of sociologist Robert Wuthnow.

I. Statistical Measures of American Christianity

From the point of view of many American religious minorities, Christianity certainly appears to be the majority faith in the United States. In fact, one might even be reminded of a cartoon of more than a decade ago, with two large fish swimming through the seas and smaller fish scampering away lest they be eaten. In the caption, one large fish says to the other, "Big fish eat little fish. I like that." From outside the tradition, American Christianity must look like a big fish that enjoys swallowing or at least intimidating smaller fish; and in truth many Americans do indeed like it that way.

Certainly more Americans identify with the term "Christian" than with any other religious term. And few would argue that the Judeo-Christian tradition has not played a crucial role in shaping American life and institutions. And yet, one hears so much about the secularization of American life and sees so much that is irreligious in American culture, that it is easy to wonder about any "Christian majority."

According to the Gallup religious preference polls, roughly 85% of Americans still claim a preference for Catholic or Protestant Christianity. Gallup polls since the 1950s indicate that the percentage of the population identifying themselves as Protestant has dropped, from 67% to 57%, but the percentage identifying with Catholicism has risen, from 25% to 28%. Meanwhile Jewish identification has dropped from 4% to 2%, while other faiths have risen from 1% to 4%.[1] George Gallup, Jr. himself says that "over the last 54 years of scientific polling, religion in America has been remarkably stable, both in . . . religious beliefs and practices."[2] The point is well taken.

Much of the talk about the decline of American religion is based on careless, and sometimes downright mischievous, use of data. For example, the apparent decline of religious indicators since the 1950s is deceptive. Although church and synagogue membership peaked at 75% in 1947, since 1975 it has hovered between 68% and 71%, roughly the same as the 72% of the late 1930s. When Gallup asks Americans, "did you, yourself, happen to attend church or synagogue in the last seven days?", about 41% say "yes," as they have since the early 1970s. That number is indeed down from a peak or 49% in 1955, but it is the same as in 1939, and it is higher than the 37% of 1940.

So in areas like religious membership and attendance at religious activities, the last fifty years have been years of stability, not unchecked decline. In fact, religious belief in America continues to astound us, particularly when we compare ourselves with other western industrialized democracies. At least 94% of Americans believe in God or a Universal Spirit. Seven in ten believe the Bible to be the Word of God; four of those seven believe it to be without errors. Seventy percent believe in life after death, compared with 45% in Great Britain, 39% in West Germany, and 25% in Denmark. Seven in ten believe in heaven, although only five-and-a-half in ten believe in hell. And 70% of Americans claim to believe that Jesus is God, a figure down slightly from the 74% of 1952.

Gallup likes to ask, do you know who gave the Sermon on the Mount, can you name all four of the Gospels, and where was Jesus born? In 1954, about 34% knew who gave the Sermon on the Mount and could name the four Gospels; by 1982 the figure had risen to about 44%. The percentage that knows Jesus' birthplace fell from 74% to a still high 70%.

Despite the evidence for stability, most Americans probably think of America as less religious than it once was, and that may be right. The anomaly is that in many ways this nation is more secular than it once was. Many sociologists cling to the secularization thesis, which argues that as society become more modern it becomes more secular, religious beliefs become privatized, and religion becomes marginalized. While there is much room to argue against this thesis (in America, thinkers have been predicting this for at least 200 years), it is not rooted solely in the biases of secular-minded, modern sociologists. Indeed, what has many Christians worried is that these sociologists may be on to something.[3]

Some figures will illustrate the point. Since the 1950s, the age of Americans claiming no religious preference has risen from 2% to 9%. In effect, the openly secular portion of the population has increased greatly.

This, coupled with the identification of many religious people with the secular values of the broader culture, has meant that secularism has indeed grown in America, mostly at the expense of more liberal religious traditions. Consequently, secularism and deep religious commitment flourish side-by-side.

Just how religious is the religious majority? Gallup's 1987 report on religion provides one answer. When people were asked for their religious preference, their religious affiliation, whether they had attended a church/synagogue in the last week, and whether religion was very important in their lives, only 4% gave negative answers to all four questions: that is, they had no religious preference, held no membership in a religious body, had not attended a service in the last week, and said that religion was not very important in their lives. Twenty-eight percent said they were neither a member of a religious body nor had attended a church/synagogue in the previous week. A full 72% claimed either religious membership or attendance at a church service in the last week.

That sounds high, but the percentage that claimed to be members of a religious body, had attended a service in the last week, and said religion was very important in their lives was only 31%, a large percentage, but a minority. If one accepts these figures, the proportion of the population that identifies itself as Christian is still an overwhelming 85% majority. But a much smaller percentage actively participate, and the difference between active and non-active can be very important.

Another reason for concern about Christianity has been the numerical decline of certain major Protestant families. Of the five major Protestant families, only Baptists have held their own in the last twenty-odd years of Gallup poll religious identification surveys, while Baptists fluctuated between 19% and 21%, the other four fell: Methodists from 14% to 9%, Lutherans from 7% to 5%, Presbyterians from 6% to 2%, and Episcopalians from 3% to 2%. Consequently, Southern Baptist identification alone is greater than that for all Methodist groups, and indeed outnumbers identification with Lutherans, Presbyterians, and Episcopalians combined.

This shift is a source of major concern to just about everyone except Southern Baptists. Of the major communities of faith from the early 1950s, only Baptists and Roman Catholics have held their percentage of the population; Catholics may have grown by a point or two. Now identification polls can exaggerate the strength of large bodies, but the others still have declined significantly, both as a percentage of the population and in real numbers. So if there is a Christian majority, it has been shaken and to some extent rearranged in the last quarter century.

II. The Restructuring of American Religion

Princeton sociologist Robert Wuthnow refers to these changes as the "restructuring of American religion."[4] American Christianity remains strong, but it is diverse, and it faces a stiff challenge from secularism and non-Christian faiths. The religious landscape has changed significantly, even if total religious commitment has not.

What does this landscape look like? It does not much resemble the picture we painted of it in the 50s, when mainline American religion was often summarized in three words: Protestant, Catholic, Jew. Using those three categories today, one would find little variety or controversy. On a host of issues there appear to be few serious differences among them anymore.

But sociologists have learned that clumsy categories like Protestant and Catholic obscure a world of tremendous variety and diversity. What Martin Marty predicted of religion in the 1980s will be true of the 1990s: religion will be everywhere, but it will be nowhere in particular. Consequently, sociologists look for new ways of organizing the diversity of mainline American religion into a coherent pattern.

One useful, though imperfect, schematic has been provided by Roof and McKinney, in their noted book, *American Mainline Religion: Its Changing Shape and Future*. They divide mainline religion into socio-religious groups, combining dozens of religious traditions into a half-dozen bodies. In descending order, ranked by size, they are: Catholics (25%), Moderate Protestants (24.2%), Conservative Protestants (15.8%), Black Protestants (9.1%), Liberal Protestants (8.7%), and Jews (2.3%). These groups differ in important and revealing ways.[5]

Of the five Christian groups, Catholics, conservative Protestants, and black Protestants rate much higher than liberal or moderate Protestants in church attendance, denominational commitment, and actual membership in a religious organization (as opposed to merely identifying with a faith). The one exception to this pattern is that actual church membership for those calling themselves Catholic is not particularly high. (One should note that Mormons and Jehovah's Witnesses "out-attend" all three of these groups).[6]

In socio-economic terms, Catholics are as likely to be middle- or upper-class as the population as a whole, while conservative and black Protestants are less likely, and moderate and liberal Protestants are more likely to be middle- or upper-class. In educational attainment, Catholics again reflect the national average, while conservative and black Protestants lag behind it, and liberal and moderate Protestants are well ahead of it.[7]

These groups differ significantly in their growth or decline. Roof and McKinney's liberal Protestants--Episcopalians, the United Church of Christ, and Presbyterians--have been losing members for decades now. To a lesser degree, so have the moderate Protestants, the Methodists, Lutherans, Disciples of Christ, and Northern Baptists. Meanwhile conservative Protestants have grown in number, if not in total percentage of the population. Why?

Conservative Protestants are clearly more active in converting others to Christianity than are liberal and moderate Protestants. Roof and McKinney also argue that the age-distribution and higher birth-rate among conservative Protestants, as compared with liberal and moderate Protestants, have and will continue to fuel these disparities in growth.

People who switch from one group to another or move outside the church altogether add an interesting dimension to the problem. Although liberal Protestants appear to gain some "switchers," these new members are typically less active than the switchers they replaced, while switchers to conservative Protestant groups tend to be as active as those they replace. In other words, the net effect of switching is to weaken liberal and moderate Protestant groups further and to strengthen conservative Protestant groups.

The greatest problem for liberal Protestants is their losses to the unaffiliated category. As Roof and McKinney put it: "the challenge to liberal Protestantism comes not so much from the conservative faiths as from the growing secular drifts of their no-so-highly committed members." Liberal Protestants and Catholics show particularly high losses of those under age forty-five, but the group most adversely affected by switching is moderate Protestants.[8]

Roof and McKinney find significant variations among these five groups regarding civil liberties, racial integration, sexual mores, and women's rights. On interracial socializing and integrated neighborhoods, conservative Protestants stand out for their low scores. In willingness to grant civil liberties to groups with unpopular ideologies, liberal Protestants rate much higher and conservative Protestants rate much lower than their counterparts.

After looking at various social and political issues, Roof and McKinney divided the religious spectrum into five categories, from the most liberal to the most conservative. At the farthest left are Jews and the unaffiliated; next come liberal Protestants, with Catholics and moderate Protestants making up the center. Black Protestants are more conservative, and conservative Protestants are the most conservative of all.[9]

It is especially noteworthy that switchers reinforce these differences, they do not dilute them, because switchers tend to share the social and moral values of those whom they are joining. The differences become sharper still if one focuses only on active participants in these traditions, factoring out the inactive, who tend to be closer to the middle of the spectrum than are their more active counterparts.

Roof and McKinney predict continued growth among black and conservative Protestants, continued decline among moderate and liberal Protestants, and sharpening divisions between the groups. Although they refrain from making predictions about Catholicism, sociologist Horace Greeley argues that much of the alleged disaffection from Catholicism has been the result of the age-distribution of American Catholics--what looks like people leaving in droves is actually young people leaving and slowly returning, a perfectly natural occurrence. Greeley concedes widespread lay disagreement with the Papacy, but suggests that American Catholics have reacted to this not so much by leaving the church as by giving less. In his words, "The laity voted not with their feet but with their checkbooks." For the immediate future, things look good, because so many Catholics appear determined to remain loyal. Greeley puts it this way:

> As I read the data and listen to the laity, I draw the following conclusion: There is nothing more the Vatican, the bishops or we priests can do to drive the laity out of the Church. We did everything we could--and often continue to do it--and still they won't go.

He and his colleague Michael Hout believe that

> the impact of sexual teaching and institutional authority on Catholic behavior is spent and that should church attendance decline again it will be for some other reason, a reason that is difficult at this time to imagine.[10]

If all of these predictions come to pass, Christianity's share of the population should hold steady or decline slightly, and it will become more conservative.

III. Basic Cleavages Within American Christianity

This brings us back to Robert Wuthnow, who suggests that the basic cleavage within American Christianity transcends these categories and denominational boundaries. The fundamental division, he says, is between evangelical and liberal Christianity. Wuthnow writes,

> the major divisions in American religion now revolve around an axis of liberalism and conservatism rather than denominational landmarks of the past. The new

> division parallels the ideological cleavage that runs through American politics. It divides religious practitioners from one another over questions of social welfare, defense spending, communism, and the so-called politics of abortion, sex education, gender equality, and prayer in public schools. But this division is not only political; it is deeply religious as well.[11]

If you ask Americans whether they are evangelicals, about 33% will say "yes."[12] If asked whether they are liberal or conservative Christians, they split, 43% liberal and 41% conservative. And the differences between the two groups intensify with exposure to one another.[13]

Wuthnow does not argue that evangelicalism or fundamentalism have experienced a revival, as some claim. But he does note that they are now better organized, and that because government has intruded more and more into the public sector, with little likelihood of backing out, there is little reason to believe that religious-political conflicts will diminish.

There are serious implications here for Muslims. Liberal Christians are more likely to tolerate or embrace those of other faiths, but they are less likely to share the strong moral and social values of traditional Islam. Conversely, conservative Christians may share Islam's strong social and moral values, but they are less likely to accept Islam as a legitimate alternative to Christianity, because conservatives are more likely than liberals to cling to the traditional Christian doctrine that salvation is attainable only through belief in a divine Jesus Christ. All other paths are thereby false paths. This makes evangelicals both more determined to convert others AND less tolerant of other faiths. What liberals call proselytizing, conservatives call evangelism. One can grow up in evangelical churches without ever hearing the word "proselytize" much less knowing what it means.

Admittedly, our age has witnessed the weakening of many institutional divisions within Christianity. The various recent mergers involving Presbyterians, Methodists, or Lutheran groups comes to mind immediately, as do the extensive dialogues conducted between Catholics, Episcopalians, and Lutherans. But much of the talk of merger and reconciliation may miss the point. Sinking ships can merge and still sink. The real gulf in Christendom today lies not between Catholics and Protestants, but between liberals and conservatives. And the conflict between those two will become more intense as the avowedly secular portion of our society continues to grow.

It should be clear now that there is not one Christian majority in America, but at least and perhaps several Christian pluralities of various strengths. Each has a claim on the American value system; each wishes decisively to influence American civil religion, that public mix of religious and political values which at the broadest level unites many Americans.

In times of conflict, cultural outsiders often suffer more than the chief combatants, but because none of these Christian groups can claim a true majority, they will need allies, and they know it. One has only to think of the enormous contribution of Jews and Mormons to recent American politics to see civil religion's potential for incorporating new faiths. As a nation, we face fundamental questions about the role of religion in the public sphere; the answers to these questions will be as important to Muslims as they are to Christians.

ENDNOTES

[1]Except where otherwise noted, the data in these paragraphs are drawn from the Gallup Religion in America reports of 1984 and 1987. More detailed data can be gleaned from Gallup's *Emerging Trends*.

[2]Quoted in *Christianity Today* (November 17, 1989):23.

[3]For a brief explanation of this thesis and some recent counters to it, see Thomas Robbins and Dick Anthony (eds.), *In Gods We Trust: New Religious Patterns of Pluralism in America* (2nd ed.; New Brunswick, N.J., 1990).

[4]Robert Wuthnow, *The Restructuring of American Religions: Society and Faith since World War II* (Princeton, N.J., 1988).

[5]William Clark Roof and William McKinney, *American Mainline Religion: Its Changing Shape and Future* (New Brunswick, N.J., 1987), 82. Roof and McKinney's data relies heavily on the General Social Survey. See their "Appendix," 253-56.

[6]Roof & McKinney, 83-84, 101.

[7]Ibid., 112-13.

[8]Ibid., 170-71.

[9]Ibid., 224.

[10]Horace Greeley, "Why Catholics Stay in the Church," in *America* 157 (1987). This article is reprinted in Robbins and Anthony, *In Gods We Trust*, 177-83. See also Horace Greeley and Michael Hout, "Musical Chairs: Patterns of Denominational Change," *American Sociological Review* 72 (1987), 75-86.

[11]Robert Wuthnow, *The Struggle for America's Soul: Evangelicals, Liberals, & Secularism* (Grand Rapids, MI, 1989), 178.

[12]*Religion in America*, The Gallup Report (April 1987/No. 259):28.

[13]Wuthnow, *The Struggle for America's Soul*, 23.

SUGGESTIONS FOR FURTHER READING

Bellah, Robert N., et al. *Habits of the Heart: Individualism and Commitment in American Life*. New York, 1985.

Fowler, Robert Booth. *Unconventional Partners: Religion and Liberal Culture in the United States*. Grand Rapids, MI, 1989.

Greeley, Andrew M. *The Catholic Myth: The Behavior and Beliefs of American Catholics*. New York, 1990.

THOMAS TEMPLETON TAYLOR is Assistant Professor of History at Wittenberg University. He received his Ph.D. in History from the University of Illinois (1988).

THE INTEGRATION OF JEWS INTO AMERICAN SOCIETY

Harold S. Himmelfarb

In this essay I would like to highlight selected aspects of Jewish integration into American society, and to suggest some possible implications for the future of the immigrant Muslim community.

When we look at Jews as a minority in the United States, we can only be impressed by the extent to which they have become well integrated into the economic and social structure of American society, and by the extent to which they have become politically influential as individuals and as an organized community. In recent decades they have become more self-consciously influential about particularly Jewish concerns in ways that were not true before the late 1960s--in ways that indicate, I think, a more comfortable psychological integration into American life.

Historically, we tend to speak of Jewish immigration to the United States as occurring in three different waves. The earliest wave was started by the immigration of Sephardic Jews from Spain and Portugal, which began around 1654 and dominated Jewish life in this country until about 1850. The second wave was that of the German Jewish immigrants, which is typically dated from about 1850 to about 1880, even though it seems that the Sephardic Jews were no longer numerically superior by as early as 1720. In fact, it is interesting to note that cultural dominance is not simply a matter of numbers; for example, even though the Sephardic Jews were already a minority by 1720, the first German Jewish synagogue was not established in the United States until 1795. Beginning around 1880 until about 1917, the third large wave of Jewish immigration occurred, composed of Jews mostly from Russia, Poland, and other Eastern European countries.

Each of these immigrations was quickly upwardly mobile in the United States, but none of them without hardship and discrimination. The small numbers and scattered presence of early Sephardic Jews did not pose much of a threat to the dominant groups in America. Nevertheless, as was true in European countries, in the colonies there were restrictions on Jews with regard to ownership of land and property, and they had to take on middleman occupations, in trade and, particularly useful at that time, in international shipping. Many of the early colonial Jews amassed wealth because they were willing to go into riskier businesses and to invest in new technologies and innovations.

The German Jews essentially saved Sephardic Jewry as a cultural entity because they infused the community with new people and new vitality. Much has been written about the wealthy German elite who established large businesses in this country and also the intellectual elites who came to this country with an ideological vision based on reformed Judaism. But most German immigrants were not educated intellectuals and most did not become extremely wealthy industrialists. Many of them worked hard to eke out a living. These Jews, like those before them, were willing to engage in riskier occupations. It was the good fortune of German Jews to come when the frontier was expanding, and many of them were willing to venture into the hinterland to peddle their goods, or set up stores, restaurants, or inns for lodging.

The Eastern European Jews came so quickly and in such great numbers that they overwhelmed the previous Jewish community, both numerically and eventually culturally. Marital desertion, poverty, and crime were not uncommon in the ghettos of the early Eastern Europeans. In fact, one of the chiefs of police in New York City in the early 1900s wrote (even if mistakenly) that half of the crimes in New York were being committed by the Jews. Nevertheless, they were able to be upwardly mobile in a short period of time because they had the talent, the motivation, and the opportunity.

The extensive writings about the factors associated with Jewish mobility in the United States have given rise to a debate between those who argue that mobility was a product of cultural values (i.e., values such as hard work, family, and especially education) and those who argue that it was due to structural factors (i.e., arriving with the right skills at the right time). While acknowledging that Jewish immigrants were typically less wealthy than other immigrants who arrived at the same time, the structuralists argue that they were more likely to have been literate (either in German or Yiddish or in the language of their country of origin), and that being literate allowed them then to learn another language more easily than, say, Italian immigrants. They were more urban-oriented; they had some experience with industrial occupations such as the textile trades and the garment industry, which were growing at that time; and they were more likely to feel that the move to the United States was permanent. Many non-Jewish immigrants thought that they were coming here for a short period of time and that they would amass some wealth and then go back to their homelands. Jewish immigrants were fleeing persecution; they came here with the notion that this was where they were going to make a home--this was where they were going to stay. In addition, Jews, particularly

Eastern European Jews, encountered an institutional framework of Jewish philanthropic and defense organizations established in order to ease their assimilation.

I find this debate unnecessary because it is not an either/or question. In fact, certain values and cultural experiences allowed Jews to make the best use of the structural opportunities that existed. However, the amount of opportunity available was dependent on the receptivity of the majority population, and its willingness to accept Jews and allow them maximum use of the opportunities that existed.

Anti-Jewish feelings and discrimination have existed throughout the Jewish experience in the United States. Peter Stuyvestant, who was the governor of the new colony which eventually became New York, had such a particular aversion to Jews that he asked the Dutch West Indies Company not to allow them to come to the United States so that they would not further affect the colonies.

In the 1920s, when Jews began to attend Harvard University in great numbers, Stuyvestant's sentiment was echoed by the University President's concern that they were affecting Harvard's cultural character (meaning the WASP--White Anglo-Saxon Protestant--character). It was not only Harvard. Harvard became the preeminent case, but there were already quotas at Columbia, Princeton, Yale, and many other places.

Nevertheless, the anti-Semitism experienced in America has been different from the anti-Semitism experienced by Jews in Europe. First, Jews in America have never been assigned any separate formal political status. Formally, they have had the same rights as all other citizens; so discrimination, to the extent that it existed, was generally covert and couched in other terms. It had no legal legitimacy. Second, anti-Semitism in the U.S. has been different because there has never been a state religion in the United States that has been able to claim dominance or require conversion. Furthermore, in colonial America, while various Protestant groups that had settled particular colonies did not like Jews, they also did not like each other very much; other Christian groups were numerically a greater threat. Thus, their own rivalries helped to diffuse what I think might have been a unified feeling of Christians against Jews. Indeed one can make the case that various attempts to restrict Catholic immigration and Catholic mobility were much more severe than anything the Protestants attempted to do to the Jews in this country.

According to recent survey data, negative stereotypes of Jews have diminished greatly in the United States, but they have not disappeared. Although about a quarter of the American public still hold latent anti-Semitic attitudes about Jews, the proportion was once much larger. About a fifth of the American public think that Jews have too much power in the

United States, and that proportion has remained steady for about the last ten years. However, if we look back to 1945, nearly sixty percent of the American public believed that Jews had too much power in the United States. Moreover, when the question is left open-ended, even fewer Americans mention Jews as a group of people who are too powerful, and more of them are likely to mention Asians, Blacks, or the Catholic Church.

There also seems to be a kind of volatile connection between events in the Middle East and anti-Semitism. When American attitudes toward Israeli policies are negative, American Jewish support for Israel is perceived negatively. But overall, American public support for Israel remains positive, and negative attitudes toward American Jews tend to fall back to earlier levels when relevant events lose their currency.

Explicit anti-Semitism does exist in the United States among the hard-core fringe, which, depending on how it is measured, may be one-half to five percent of the population. There are pockets, or segments, of the economy which are still notorious for isolating and keeping Jews out. In recent times, Jews have been concerned about what they perceive as anti-Semitic media coverage of Jewish problems, and particularly of Israel. (Undoubtedly, the Muslim community perceives it differently.)

One particular, and ironic, media-related problem deserves mention. American Jews have typically portrayed themselves and the Israelis as the underdog; but now that Jews are an influential, affluent community in the United States, and Israel is a powerful military force, the underdog image with which the media has liked to identify has become less supportable.

There is also what some people have called a new anti-Semitism about, which is really less of an anti-Semitism than a callousness to Jewish issues. Media coverage is one example. Public discourse about Jews is another. Certain kinds of public language which were not acceptable twenty years ago are now becoming more acceptable, as in the 1984 Presidential campaign of Jesse Jackson. Most repugnant of all is the revisionist school of history which argues that the Holocaust never occurred. This is found not only in the United States but in Europe, where it began and continues.

There are new issues for American Jews as a minority in the United States. Since the late 1960s, the primary concerns of the organized Jewish community have shifted from promoting Jewish socio-economic mobility toward promoting Jewish culture and Jewish identification. This shift has caused, among other things, a new particularism within the Jewish community. Politically, particularism has been good for American Jews because it has enabled them to be proactive rather than defensive with regard to Jewish issues. Two such issues are Israel and Soviet Jewry.

The irony here is that the shift toward particularism has allowed these issues to become central ones on the Jewish communal agenda, but the success in obtaining wider support for these causes has been due to the community's ability to couch the issues in universalistic terms--Israel in terms of promoting democracy, and Soviet Jewry in terms of promoting human rights.

The more particularistic focus of the community has raised questions about the validity of some long-held principles, such as the need to maintain a very clear line between Church and State (a line which, in fact, has always been unclear). Jews have fought hard to maintain the separation of the two, feeling that their interests as a religious minority could thrive only when government was not involved with religion. Today, however, feeling more secure in their status as American citizens and more concerned about perpetuating Jewish continuity, some Jewish groups are beginning to challenge the wisdom of this principle, particularly as it applies to government support of religious day-schools, and the promotion of religion and religious values as a social good.

What are the implications of all this for Muslims? First, as it exists in the United States today, religious pluralism creates advantages for Muslims as well as for Jews. The two communities can work together to encourage more of that, for example, to defend against what some perceive as a kind of evangelical thrust, exemplified by the Christian fundamentalist right, which has begun more and more to define American society as a Christian society in very vocal and explicit terms.

Muslims in the United States might feel that there is a greater public sensitivity to Jewish concerns than there is to Muslim concerns, but some of that lack of sensitivity will undoubtedly disappear in time. In comparison to American Jews, Muslims are a much more recent immigrant group, and the American public has not yet become aware of who they are, how many they are, and what their concerns are.

All societies affect the religious groups within them, and societies change the way that religious traditions--no matter how tied to sacred texts--manifest themselves. One of the things that has happened to American Judaism, which might have implications for the Muslim faith in the United States, is that differences among Jews have shifted from being based on ethnic differences (i.e., cultural differences stemming from different countries of origin) to internal differences based on ideology.

Religion in this Protestant country is characteristically denominational, and Jews have followed that model. There are now four separate Jewish denominations, and significant ideological differences have developed among this group of people who identify themselves as belonging to the same faith. There have also been some strong structural differences that have occurred due to the encounter with American society, so that, for example, there are denominational differences in the amount of praying in English rather than in Hebrew, and in the extent of female participation and leadership that has been sanctioned.

The thing that unites Jews in this country, given that they do have ideological differences about faith, is a common concern about Jewish welfare, here and abroad. This manifests itself in the strong concern of American Jews for Israel. In fact, survey data indicate that there is more support for the notion of a secure Israel than there is for any kind of theological issue, perhaps even the notion of one God.

This really means that American Jews, although they recognize themselves as a religious group, actually participate in an ethnic way, as a single people rather than as a single religion. The presence of this strong ethnic dimension of Jewish identity may be the main difference between American Jews and American Muslims. It may also explain some of the tension that will probably exist between the two groups as long as there is not peace in the Middle East, and as long as Israel remains one of the major unifying factors for American Jews.

However, there is a new factor in American Jewry's relationship to Israel that contains another lesson with possible implications for American Muslims. Given their new feeling of security both within this country and as a community, and given their developing relationship with Israeli society, American Jews now feel that their role toward Israel is not just one of support. Now they feel that they also have, or ought to have, a voice in what Israel does. This has meant that American Jewry occasionally tries to play a moral role of reminding the Jewish state that its political policies and actions ought to be in accord with time-honored Jewish values. I would suggest the American Muslim community could play the same role with regard to its fellow-Muslims across the seas, drawing on both American and Islamic ideals of tolerance for groups with different practices and beliefs.

SUGGESTIONS FOR FURTHER READING

Feingold, Henry L. *A Midrash on American Jewish History*. Albany, 1982.

Liebman, Charles S., and Steven M. Cohen. *Two Worlds of Judaism: The Israeli and American Experiences*. New Haven, 1990.

Quinley, Harold E., and Charles Y. Glock. *Anti-Semitism in America*. New York, 1979.

Waxman, Chaim I. *America's Jews in Transition*. Philadelphia, 1983.

HAROLD S. HIMMELFARB is Associate Professor of Sociology at The Ohio State University and Senior Research Associate at the Office of Educational Research and Improvement, U.S. Department of Education. He received his Ph.D. in Sociology of Education from The University of Chicago (1974).

The views expressed here are those of the author, and no official support by the U.S. Department of Education is intended or should be inferred.

MUSLIMS LIVING NEXT DOOR

Ilyas Ba-Yunus

When Will Herberg published his *Protestant-Catholic-Jew* in 1960, he informed us that "95% of the American people, according to a recent public opinion survey, declared themselves to be either Protestants, Catholics, or Jews (68 percent Protestants, 23 percent Catholics, 4 percent Jews); only 5 percent admitted to 'no preference.'" Should he choose to write the same book today, Herberg would probably change its title to *Protestant-Catholic-Jew-Muslim*, because the demographic landscape of American religion has changed drastically during the intervening years.

From almost a statistical non-entity in 1960, Muslim population, according to various estimates, now stands between three and six million in the U.S. alone; if we add the number of Muslims residing in Canada, the population of Muslims in North America could possibly be in the neighborhood of eight million, or slightly higher than three percent of the total North American population. If its growth rate remains the same, the Muslim population of North America could conceivably reach ten million by the year 2000.

I. History

Clearly, the decade of the 1960s may be taken as a turning point in the demographic history of Muslims in North America. No one knows when the first Muslims set foot on the North American continent. Eleventh- and twelfth-century world maps prepared by Muslim geographers show the existence of large islands to the northwest of Europe. This has prompted some Muslim scholars, such as M. Hamidullah of France, to speculate that the Muslim explorers had already discovered Iceland and Greenland at least two centuries before Columbus set sail across the Atlantic. Still others maintain that some of the long-bearded sailors who accompanied Columbus were Mesopotamians who, according to M. Salahuddin of Cambridge, were convinced that across the Bahr Zulmat (the Sea of Darkness) there was another world with its own civilization. If these constitute mere speculations, it is estimated with some certainty that fourteen to twenty percent of the West Africans captured and sold as slaves in America were

Muslim. Alex Haley's *Roots* is based on similar folklore among contemporary African-Americans in the United States.

The very first officially recorded information about Muslims in North America is to be found in the California State Archives, which show the existence of a large number of farm laborers of Indian origin. These Indian laborers were first brought to British Columbia in the middle of the nineteenth century. By the turn of the century, these laborers had already migrated south to settle in northern California's Stockton Valley. These laborers included Muslim and Sikh workers from the Punjab in British India. Descendants of the Punjabi Muslims (from what is now Pakistan) are still to be found in large numbers around Sacramento, Stockton, and the Bay area, where they have prospered, many working as middlemen.

While the Punjabi Muslims settled down on the West coast, the East coast of the United States was receiving Muslim immigrants of Arab, Turkish, and Albanian origin. M. Elkholey of Northern Illinois University and S.S. Nyang of Howard University have written extensively on these Middle Eastern Muslim immigrants who continued to trickle in the United States until 1950s. However, nobody, not even these two eminent students of Islam in America, could give an estimate as to the size of the Muslim population on this continent during the 1950s.

In 1967, the Muslim Students Association of U.S. and Canada commissioned me to devise a plan for the census of the Muslim population. In the course of doing this, it was discovered that the Federation of the Islamic Associations in America (FIAA) had shown the same interest in a Muslim census in 1960 and that it had requested its affiliates to enumerate their respective populations. Instead these communities enumerated the number of households within their jurisdictions, producing a total of 187,000 households belonging to the Muslim associations under the umbrella of the FIAA. Because not all of them had responded to the request of the FIAA, the estimate of the number of the households was upgraded and rounded out at 200,000. Multiplying this by a rough estimate of the average family size, i.e., six, one arrived at a rough estimate of the Muslim population at about 1,200,000, certainly not less than one million in 1960. Our computations show that this population has been expanding at the rate of two percent per year, which is much higher than the American average, but almost the same as the world average today. Islam may in fact be the most rapidly increasing religious affiliation in North America.

Reasons for the phenomenal growth of the Muslim population in subsequent years are many. Immigration and natural growth are the most important; conversion is a distant third.

Since the 1960s there has been a great deal of conversion to Islam. African-Americans have been especially drawn by Islam's color blindness, its egalitarianism, and its insistence on brotherhood and sisterhood among the believers. This has been truer since the death in 1975 of Elijah Muhammad, the leader of the Nation of Islam. Two of his sons who were educated at Al-Azhar University in Cairo had already accepted orthodox Islam. After their father's death, almost the whole following of Elijah Muhammad adopted his son Wallace Muhammad's lead. Moreover, coversion to Islam among African-Americans is a continuous process. Especially those who are incarcerated in prisons find a great deal of much needed group-support by accepting Islam. In several prisons that I have visited, Muslim inmates are particularly conspicuous in providing support and other services to their Muslim fellow-inmates.

We do not know how many African-Americans have accepted Islam over the years. However, a cursory look at several Muslim communities around the continent shows that the numbers who are visiting mosques regularly and participating in community affairs is increasing. Some of them appear to be practicing polygamy and to have large families. In conversation, their Imams estimate the number of African-American Muslims at one million, but the basis for the estimate is difficult to ascertain.

More important is immigration. The Johnson administration adopted an open immigration policy in 1964. Soon the Canadian government followed suit. The very first beneficiaries of this immigration policy were about 100,000 students who were studying in American and Canadian universities and colleges. A sizeable number of them were from the Middle East and other Muslim areas. However, the number of students seeking immigration in this continent was only a small fraction of the potential immigrants who deluged American and Canadian embassies in Pakistan, India, Malaysia, Indonesia, Taiwan, the Philippines, South Korea, and various Middle Eastern, African, and South American countries. Soon after they were legally admitted to this continent, they received their citizenship; and no sooner had they received their citizenship than they sponsored for immigration their immediate relatives (parents, brothers, sisters, and the spouses).

Thus, although open immigration was tightened in 1971 and then abolished in 1975, those who were already legally admitted continued to sponsor new immigrants. This resulted in an inverse pyramidal progression in immigration. Each person who was admitted legally was entitled to sponsor two parents, a number of brothers and sisters, and their spouses and their children. I alone was able to sponsor twenty-one legal immigrants, each of whom received his or her relatives, who in their turn will carry this process further unless the laws of immigration are changed drastically.

Immigration, then, has been the largest contributor to the phenomenal growth in Muslim population in this continent since the 1960s. Because no change in the existing laws of immigration is in sight, legal immigration of Muslims in this continent promises to continue indefinitely. Once one becomes a citizen, one is given the right to and shall sponsor kith and kin as long as they are eager to migrate.

Natural growth, i.e., birth minus death, has also contributed significantly. While the death-rate of Muslim immigrants must have gone down appreciably (compared with what it would have been had they remained in their countries of origin), it is doubtful that their birth-rate has declined significantly in North America; and the combination of relatively high birth-rate and a declining death-rate is a recipe for population explosion.

II. Distribution

The Muslim population explosion has been accompanied by the diffusion and expansion of Muslim commmunal life. When I came to the University of Minnesota in 1960, as a graduate student, there were no Muslims living in the twin cities of Minneapolis and St. Paul except for a handful of students in or around the university campuses. Now the twin cities boast three mosques which serve a population of almost four hundred families. Similar changes have been reported in Houston, Miami, Seattle, Kansas City, or Nashville. Until 1960, Muslims were living in large metropolitan areas such as New York, Philadelphia, Washington D.C., Chicago, Detroit, and Los Angeles, and in some smaller communitites in Indiana, Iowa, Michigan, New Jersey, the Stockton Valley in California, and in or around Toronto and Edmonton in Canada.

Today, a cursory glance at the membership list of the Islamic Society of North America shows that nearly all the cities in this continent with a population of 100,000 or more had a large number of Muslim families residing for quite some time. Even smaller towns such as Muncie, Indiana; Athens, Ohio; Winona, Minnesota; Martin, Tennesse; Gainseville, Florida; Cortland, New York, Springfield, Massachusetts; Cedar Rapids, Iowa; Fort Collins, Colorado; Moscow, Idaho; and Kingston, Ontario have several Muslim families residing on a more or less permanent basis.

This distribution of the Muslim population shows that although most Muslims, like most other new immigrants, prefer to live in large metropolitan areas, they have been spilling over into smaller towns, many of which are situated in the middle of farming and rural areas. This expansion reflects two traits: 1) the confidence and aggressiveness with which Muslims moved into uncharted territories, apparently undeterred by potential ethnic and religious intolerance on the part of the local populations; 2) the unusual talent and services Muslims can render to the local populations.

III. Accomplishments

Unlike those previous immigrants who came to this continent as poorly educated people trying to escape poverty in their respective lands, recent Muslim immigrants generally came either as graduate students, as well trained professionals, or as experienced small businessmen. Consequently, the Muslim whom one is likely to encounter these days is most often a medical doctor, an engineer, an accountant, a college professor, or a businessman. Because of the high rate of urbanization in the U.S. and Canada, a professional void was created in smaller towns and rural areas; and Muslim professionals were happy to fill these gaps as long as they were received like any other professionals.

Such educational and professional status paid an average Muslim immigrant high dividends, such as a general standard of living much higher than in his home country, but also much higher than that of the average American. Those who work in large metropolitan areas often live in commutable suburbs. Those who live in smaller towns have homes in relatively prosperous neighborhoods with good schooling facilities for their children, most of whom have been born in this continent and speak American English fluently.

Because of a relatively high educational level and consciousness in the family, the Muslim student has been able to do very well in schools and colleges. Like the children of many other immigrant parents, an average Muslim child is often close to the top of his or her class. In this respect, living in a good school district is a big help, but there also seems to be something in immigration that makes children relatively more achievement-oriented.

A closer look at the immigrant Muslim family shows that Muslim parents 1) are themselves quite educated, 2) spend a relatively greater amount of time at home with their children, and 3) are relatively more concerned and actively help their children more in solving their educational problems. The average Muslim family is more stable and more family-oriented. Alcoholism, parental fights, divorce, and other problems which demoralize the average American family are rare. Consequently, the high achievement-orientation of an average Muslim student is further reinforced by the development of self-confidence, a sense of security, and a stable personality. In short, the average Muslim immigrant in the first generation is the epitome of the American success story, and the first generation is actively transferring its strength to the next generation.

IV. Problems

Having solved their economic problems successfully, however, Muslims in North America have yet to solve the problems of settlement in a predominantly Christian society with secular values and a high desire for assimilation. Living as a minority in a non-Muslim society is not new to Muslims; for centuries there have been large Muslim minorities in India, China, Russia, Central Asia, and Eastern Europe. A number of smaller countries in Africa, South East Asia, and the Caribbean also contain sizeable Muslim minorities. In countries like China, these minorities have fared well and even prospered, economically and otherwise. In countries like India, there have been serious intercommunal conflicts. In countries where the Muslim minority has been able to assimilate without having to lose its basic faith and other practices, it has been able to survive through generations. Where assimilation is not possible or means losing basic Muslim identity, Muslim/non-Muslim relations have not been easy. Which situation will the new setting of North America provide?

The history of Muslim-Christian relations has been mixed. Before the rise of Islam, Mediterranean powers like the Roman and Byzantine empires sought to colonize and control the area now known as the Middle East. With the advent of an Islamic empire, the Middle East could no longer be controlled by powers to its west, and it also became a world power and a civilization to reckon with. During the Crusades, it became again an object of western economic and military expansion, and a focal point for religious conflict as well.

The legacy of the Crusades still poisons Muslim-Christian relations and, for that matter, Western-Middle Eastern relations. Stereotypes, lack of trust, and name-calling exist on all sides. Strange as it may sound, while the memory of the Crusades has long faded from the minds of modern generations, the negative images that the Crusades left behind persist.

Subsequent events have added to the problem, for example, the Ottoman domination of Eastern Europe (fifteenth-seventeenth centuries), the expulsion of Muslims from Christianized Spain (early seventeenth century), the colonization of the Middle East by European powers, the establishment of the state of Israel in the British Mandate of Palestine, and subsequent Palestinian attacks on easy-to-reach civilian targets in Europe and elsewhere. All of these events have refreshed and further enhanced old stereotypes.

North America is a continent largely inhabited by immigrants or their descendants. However, as successive waves of immigrants have entered this continent from different parts of the world, America has also become the site of ethnic and racial prejudice and outright discrimination. Each ethnic group which has entered the U.S. has become an object of jokes and stereotypes on the part of those who came earlier.

Muslim immigrants are the victims of double jeopardy. They are not only one of the most recent groups to arrive, but they also bring with them the negative labels attached to them through centuries of hostile relationships and perpetuated through current events. Wherever Muslims are living as conspicuous communities, as in Dearborn, Michigan; Lackwanna, New York; or Orange County, California, latent prejudice on the part of the majority erupts in the form of open slurs and even physical harm or intimidation each time there is some incident involving the Middle East and America. Some non-Muslim Americans have adopted a "Moslems are coming" mentality. There have been several incidents of attempted desecration of mosques or even arson. Naturally, these acts of vandalism are not committed by the more responsible and the more thoughtful. However, such acts, infrequent as they may be, are enough to create a siege mentality among Muslims who, having adopted a middle-class life style, often live not together but far away from one another in different neighborhoods. When their homes are vandalized, it is not difficult for them to put the blame on the whole Christian population even though most Christians oppose such acts. If assimilation of the Muslim is to take place, at the least anti-Muslim hostility, old and new stereotypes, and desecration of the mosques must stop.

Even so, how far can any one be expected to assimilate in this society? Except for the English language, which provides for a degree of assimilation, several national groups that have migrated into this society show few signs of assimilation. Even language may not always unify. For instance, there is African-American English, Hispanic English, and Caucasian English in this society. Sociological research has pointed out that more than a "melting pot," American society is like a mosaic composed of several racial, religious, ethnic, and national groups trying to create an uneasy symbiosis. It might, then, be more realistic to speak of the "Americanization" of the Muslim than of the assimilation. This symbiosis may be difficult for Muslims and non-Muslims alike. Or, it may be an easy transition. It all depends on how they come to understand each others' sensitivities, concerns, and worldviews.

V. Conclusion

Because much of the misunderstanding between Muslim and non-Muslim Americans dates back to older Muslim-Christian and Muslim-Jewish conflicts, Muslim-Christian-Jewish trialogue is a sensible first step to take. As a result, Muslims might take more to heart the Qur'an's definition of Christians and Jews as People of the Book. By the same token, Christians could focus on Muslims' utmost reverence for Jesus Christ, and on their carrying his message beyond Christendom itself. After all, the Qur'an may be the only non-Christian sacred Book that recognizes the virgin birth of Jesus Christ and his prophethood. Jews could, likewise, focus on the Muslims' belief in the prophethood of Abraham, Joseph, Moses, David, and others.

With so much in common, Jews, Christians, and Muslims would do to better forget the past and look for a better future together. Once an understanding is reached among the three peoples, more avenues for cooperation will open up. For instance, all are living in the same problem-ridden society. Divorce, crime, juvenile delinquency, pre-marital sex, adultery, and drugs plague Jews and Christians as well as Muslims in this society. When recession hits, it does not know a Christian from a Muslim. When inflation appears, it hits both Jews and Muslims. When AIDS strikes, it does not discriminate between or among religions. With so many problems to solve, it is urgent that all three communities put their heads together and develop a united front. In trying to solve these problems, it is hoped that the Christians, Jews, and Muslims will come to respect one another's dignity. As the Qur'an (109:6) says, "Your faith is for you and our faith is for us."

SUGGESTIONS FOR FURTHER READING

Bilgé, Barbara J. "Islam in the Americas." In Mircea Eliade (ed.), *The Encyclopedia of Religion*. New York, 1987, 7:425-431.

Elkholey, M. "Muslim Population in North America." *Al-Ittihad* (Spring 1967).

Hamidullah, M. *Islam*. London, 1986.

Nyang, Sulayman S. "The History of Muslim Immigration in the U.S." Paper presented to the Symposium on Muslims in North America, 1983.

Salahuddin, M. "Muslim Exploration and Mapmaking 800-1400 A.D." *Islamic Review* (May 1969).

ILYAS BA-YUNUS is Professor of Sociology at the State University of New York College at Cortland. He received his Ph.D. in Sociology from Oklahoma State University (1970).

ON-GOING MUSLIM-CHRISTIAN DIALOGUE

Stephan J. Moloney

The journey of dialogue and discovery among Muslims and Christians in the Central Ohio area began in early 1989 when Dr. Mazhar Jalil mentioned to Bishop James A. Griffin of the Catholic Diocese of Columbus the possibility of establishing a formal relationship to promote dialogue between Muslims and Christians. Bishop Griffin readily agreed to this proposal and asked me to work with Dr. Jalil and others to bring this about. To broaden the Christian dimension of this effort, the Metropolitan Area Church Board became involved, especially through the efforts of its executive director, Reverend Robert Erickson.

In my early conversation with Dr. Jalil, we discussed our vision for this dialogue, and took some cues from a successful effort in Milwaukee, Wisconsin, which was extensively covered in the publication *New Catholic World*.

On September 16, 1991, Bishop James A. Griffin, Sister Anne McCarrick, S.N.D. deN. and I were guests at the Islamic Center as we entered into a formal agreement to pursue our vision. Likewise, on behalf of the Islamic community, Sohail Khan, Acar Cener, and Dr. Jalil signed the same agreement, in which we expressed our hopes and embraced the challenge of dialogue.

In that historic agreement, we laid the philosophical foundation for our future relationship, and committed ourselves to respect. We said "Dialogue presupposes that each side wishes to know the other, and wishes to increase and deepen its knowledge of the other. It constitutes a particularly suitable means of favoring a better mutual knowledge and of probing the riches of one's own tradition. Dialogue demands respect for the other as he is; above all for his faith and his religious convictions."

During the ensuing months, preparations were made for the conference to be held in March 1990 at the Great Southern Hotel, "Muslims and Christians: Common Themes, Distinct Identities." The fruits of that event are readily evident elsewhere in this volume.

The March 1990 Conference, although the first and largest project of our dialogue, was only the beginning, as had been our intention all along. No sooner did the conference end, but Dr. Jalil and I again began to meet, along with Reverend Mike Bledsoe of First Baptist Church and Sister Anne McCarrick, S.N.D. deN., to plan the next phases of our developing relationship.

We agreed that it was of great importance to keep the dialogue "alive," that is, to maintain interest among both Muslims and Christians by sponsoring relatively frequent, informal discussions focused on specific topics.

Two such sessions have been held each year since the Conference in March 1990.

The first occurred on June 2, 1990, and concerned the topic "Law and Justice." I had the privilege of speaking on the Christian understanding of the virtue of justice and of the role of law--divine, natural, and human--for Christians. Ala Hamoudi and Abe Bahgat explained the qur'anic foundations of Islamic law and jurisprudence. This first informal dialogue, like those which were to follow, was characterized by a real eagerness to know among the participants. Lively discussions with many questions and respectful debate have been typical experiences at these sessions. Most of all, there has always been a sense of discovery as both Christians and Muslims are surprised as well by our common convictions and similar religious, spiritual, and social experiences and aspirations.

The second dialogue session following the March 1990 Conference dealt with a very practical concern: the problems raised by interfaith marriages for both Christians and Muslims. I again had the honor of speaking on this topic. I used my background in Canon Law to present how the Church has dealt with interfaith and "mixed" marriages historically and currently. Bashir Ahmed spoke eloquently of the long-standing Islamic custom permitting marriages between Muslims and Christians or Jews, the "people of the book." But by far the best insights in this session came from the spontaneous remarks and discussion among those who have expereinced the richness and the challenges of living in a Muslim-Christian marriage.

In 1991, the third dialogue since the March 1990 Conference was held on July 13. This time the topic was a comparison of our traditions of charity and fasting. Reverend Donald Franks, the former Vicar for Catholic Charities and Social Concerns, spoke very concretely about the types of charitable efforts the Catholic Church is involved in, which is similar to many other Christian denominations in this respect. He spoke of the Christian faith's tradition of embracing the poor and vulnerable. Dr. Haskin Kamali spoke of charity as one of the the five pillars of Islam.

The most recent dialogue occurred on October 26, 1991, and was devoted to the topic of holidays and traditions. On that occasion, Dr. Bashir Ahmed and Reverend Kevin Kavanagh spoke of the festival days and celebrations of Muslims and Christians respectively. Times of fasting and penance are also common to both religions.

These dialogues, the spontaneous discussion that inevitably accompany them, together with the friendly socializing that is also characteristic of these meetings, have demonstrated to all participants that Christians and Muslims have much in common, especially our values; furthermore, where differences exist, we have all learned that these are not conflicts to be resolved but unique characteristics of our respective religions to be understood, respected, and appreciated.

When the formal agreement to pursue this process of dialogue was signed back on September 16, 1989, Bishop Griffin remarked on that occasion:

> Our society is so diverse and changes so quickly that the common and enduring values that religious people of all faiths stand for must compete with contrary practices and attitudes. If, in the course of this dialogue, we Christians and Muslims can come to an understanding of our religious and ethical common ground, we will be better able to stand together, giving a common witness to the larger community in central Ohio.

The Bishop also spoke of his hope that the dialogue would not just help us to understand one another's faith and culture, but would also "cement a bond of solidarity based on the fact that we are all religious people."

Those hopes and aspirations have begun to be realized in our two years of formal and informal dialogue and interaction, and we look forward to continued growth and deepening of this relationship that promises to bear much more fruit in the future.

REVEREND STEPHAN J. MOLONEY is Vice-Chancellor of the Diocese of Columbus. He received his B.A. in English from the Pontifical College Josephinum (1978), his M.A. in Theology and M.D.V. from Mt. St. Mary's Seminary (1982 and 1986, respectively), and his Licentiate in Canon Law from the Pontifical University of St. Thomas (1988). He was ordained in 1982.

JEWISH-MUSLIM DIALOGUE IN OUR COMMUNITIES: AN IDEA AND AN OPPORTUNITY WHOSE TIME HAS COME

Harold J. Berman

In March of 1985, I received a letter from a man who was to become a cherished friend of mine and of my congregation, Dr. Mazhar Jalil, then President of the Islamic Foundation of Central Ohio. His organization, more commonly known as the Islamic Center, is the religious center for a large group of Muslims in Columbus and is located only a few buildings away from my congregation on East Broad Street in Columbus, Ohio. The letter very simply stated that Dr. Jalil would like to meet me and hoped that our meeting could foster better understanding between our communities.

I wrote back to Dr. Jalil and we soon met in my office and talked for more than an hour. Dr. Jalil spoke of his desire to have more contact with the synagogue and to be able to exchange views not only on religious questions and on common elements of our history, but also on practical issues of minority life in an American Christian society. He felt, however, that at least to begin, we should proceed slowly and with a minimum of public attention.

Several weeks later, at Dr. Jalil's invitation, we met a second time at the Islamic Center. I brought with me some of the leaders of my congregation's board and staff. Dr. Jalil, whose leadership is entirely voluntary, invited a selected group of board members and teachers to meet with us.

We discovered a community of people with whom we have a lot in common and who also felt that they have a lot in common with us. We recognized that we could learn from each other.

In many ways, a large segment of the Muslim community resembles the Jewish community of fifty or seventy-five years ago. Most of the parents are foreign-born. (However, unlike the first generation of Jews in America, a large number of them have acquired distinguished academic credentials and professional positions in America.) They are not, in many cases, politically oriented, nor do they see any likelihood of returning to their native countries.

Many of our Muslim neighbors are troubled by issues and concerns that are very familiar to the Jewish community. They very much want their children to be Americans, but they also want their children to have a strong religious identity, to know how to worship in their faith and to be familiar with its sacred texts. They worry about assimilation and intermarriage. Many spouses among them are converts. They worry about how to fit into American society without being swallowed up by it. In a discussion about Christmas it emerged that some of them, in their search for "American" ways, have Christmas trees in their homes. Their mosque is a voluntary association, and since many have come from countries where religious needs were provided by the government, collecting dues is a problem, as is the recruitment of volunteer workers. Teachers in their schools are not always able to relate well to the American-born children. I asked, in one discussion, about the teaching of Arabic in their Sunday School, and I was told that there is constant debate. Some want to teach conversational Arabic; others only want to teach Arabic for prayer and for the reading of the Qur'an. It all sounded very familiar.

We slowly began to establish programs which would be meaningful for both educational and social exchange. We have had a number of lectures in which we gathered either for a presentation by myself or by a member of the synagogue on a topic of Jewish history or religion, or for one of the leaders of the Islamic Center to speak about Muslim traditions and history. We gathered one December to talk about being minorities in a Christian society and exchanged some practical thoughts on practical issues. Each gathering involved food, usually dessert. This worked because they are very careful about ingredients and also check labels to avoid lard as a shortening. Many told us that they look for symbols of Hashgakha (Kosher supervision) to guide them as they shop.

We have also held social programs of an informal nature, just to do things together and foster the opportunity for people to know their neighbors. A picnic at the end of one summer brought about a half dozen families from each group into softball games, touch football, a chance to eat together and to hear each other recite mealtime blessings. On another occasion, we had a number of families from the Islamic Center as guests at the synagogue for a Shabbat dinner at which we explained rituals and customs. This was followed by a service at which Dr. Jalil sat on the Bimah with me and presented a Qur'an to our synagogue library as I presented a Tanakh to the Islamic Center. Each was inscribed with words of friendship.

We have gradually gone public. Dr. Jalil writes letters of greeting which we read to our congregation on Rosh Hashanah (the Jewish New Year), and I write letters of good wishes for the feast of Id al-Fitr (which ends the Islamic month of fasting). Dr. Jalil also sent a letter of condolence after the murder of worshippers at the Neve Shalom synagogue in Istanbul. It was later printed in our synagogue bulletin. Minimal publicity has gone into the newspapers, but gradually we have allowed the story to be told, and it has been greeted warmly by most members of the community. We have been invited to provide speakers for some community events and thus have shared platforms together before community groups. Dr. Jalil, a warm and generous man, a lover of peace, has become a personal friend whom I cherish.

In the spring of 1989, after months of preparation, and with funding from several public foundations, we held a major conference in Columbus, a full afternoon of presentations, lectures, discussion groups, and special greetings. Public officals were invited, publicity was extensive, and more than 300 people attended.

In order to avoid questions of bias or control, we did not use any Jewish community or any Muslim community sources of funding. We also did not meet in either of our buildings, but used a downtown hotel instead. We served a kosher lunch. We took a break for afternoon prayer, the Jews in one room and the Muslims in another, with anyone welcome at either service. It was considered by all who participated to have been a very successful day.

We hope to do more. We hope, within this year, to have a selected group of teenagers from the synagogue and the mosque sitting and studying Tanakh and Qur'an together. We hope to continue adult exchange study programs on a deeper level as well. There is much more to do.

I believe that our experience of Jewish-Muslim dialogue can be duplicated, in some form, in other communities. The exceptional personality of Dr. Jalil, certainly the most important force in our community, will not be available everywhere, but there are many other men and women of good faith who love peace, who are committed to being good neighbors in their new homes, and who are genuinely seeking models for new lifestyles in America.

We can help them, and they can help us. When, during a hostage crisis several years ago, a local newspaper ran a headline and story which seemed to equate all Muslims with terrorists and hijackers, I wrote a letter to the paper in protest. I received calls and letters from many new friends in the community and many others I did not know, thanking me for that support. Muslims join with us in speaking out against prayer in school, for greater understanding of holiday absences from work and school for religious minorities, and for minority rights in the Soviet Union.

Making the contact is the crucial beginning. It takes a long time to build up confidence, to accept the risks involved, and to learn to be grateful for what is possible and to understand what is not.

Peace is accomplished through very small tentative steps. If we start with our neighbors and share warmth and community with them, there is no way of predicting where it might lead. Some day it might make a real difference, not only in our communities but on a much larger scale in the world in which we live.

RABBI HAROLD J. BERMAN has served as spiritual leader of Congregation Tifereth Israel in Columbus, Ohio, since 1979. He received his B.A. from Rutgers University (1969), his M.A. from the Jewish Theological Seminary of America (1973), and Rabbinic Ordination, also from the Jewish Theological Seminary (1975).

AFTERWORD

Norman Hosansky
Congregation Tifereth Israel

Since the "Muslims and Jews" conference of March 19, 1989, informal contact has been maintained, and groups from the Islamic Center and Congregation Tifereth Israel have gotten together five times: once for Friday evening services at the synagogue followed by Shabbat dinner, and four times for study. The study sessions included two on the Qur'an and Sunna, focusing on the moral teachings of Islam, and two on the Tanakh, including such topics as the covenant of circumcision, the holiness code found in Deuteronomy, and the role of the prophets. The study sessions heard some lively discussion emphasizing the remarkable similarities and significant differences of our two religious traditions and their teachings.

NORMAN HOSANSKY is Chairman of the Muslim-Jewish Task Force, and retired Manager, Organic Chemistry Department, Chemical Abstracts Service. He received his Ph.D. in Chemistry from Rutgers University (1953).